GIVE OUR KIDS A REAL HEAD START

Tips On Teaching Your Kids How To Read Early
Plus Other Ways To Keep Them Ahead In Grades K-12

SAMANTHA W. DAVIS

authorHOUSE®

AuthorHouse™
1663 Liberty Drive
Bloomington, IN 47403
www.authorhouse.com
Phone: 1-800-839-8640

First published by AuthorHouse 5/16/2011

ISBN: 978-1-4567-5673-4 (sc)
ISBN: 978-1-4567-5674-1 (e)

Library of Congress Control Number: 2011904743

Printed in the United States of America

Thank You

I would like to first, thank God, who is all knowing, all powerful, the creator of all, and loving, for making this book possible. I could not have written this book without God's help, and I am forever thankful. In the book of Matthew, "26 Jesus looked at them and said, "With man this is impossible, but with God all things are possible." " *(1. Matthew 19:26 NIV)*

In addition, I would like to thank my loving and supportive husband for encouraging me to write and finish this book. I would also like to thank him for his insight and for his editorial skills. He has been with me from the start of this project. Finally yet importantly, I would like to thank my two smart and beautiful children for being the inspiration of this book. I hope this book motivates parents and teachers alike, to teach America's children how to read early, along with some other basic learning skills before starting school. Efforts like this may help stamp out adult illiteracy in our country, and put America on top again in Science, Math, and Reading.

Dedication

This book is affectionately devoted to my beautiful and loving mothers, Nancy W. Manning, Marion A. Franks, Doris L. Young, my Mother- in-law Florence Davis and my godmother Betty Mixon. They have instilled in me the fact that it's irrelevant where you start in life, but what is important-- is taking the cards you're dealt in life and winning at the game anyway...God's way.

Contents

CHAPTER I

27. "...run with patience the race
that is set before us..." Heb. 12:1-3

Introductions and Why I Wrote This Book

Thank you for buying this book! Before we get started, let's introduce ourselves. I think I know a few things about you already. You want to give your child a real head start in school. You desire to teach him/her how to read early (if your child isn't reading yet), and keep him/her ahead in grades K-12th. You also like buying books like this one, to help your kids, and you are extremely hands-on. Well, was I right? I could have left off or added a thing or two, but now that I know some things about you, let me tell you a few things about me. Well, my name is Samantha Davis, and I graduated from Florida State University with a degree in Business Marketing. I am a former daycare owner and teacher. I'm also an entrepreneur, an author, and an education advocate (...can you guess?). I am happily married with two wonderful and beautiful kids. I also taught both of them how to read by the age of three! Boy was that a mouth full!

I was thrilled that I managed to teach not one, but both of my kids how to read early. When my first child was reading by three, I was happy, but I didn't think much about it at the time. However, when both of them were reading by three, I said, "Hey, wait a minute!" That is when I got the idea that maybe I could help others do the same with their children. Nonetheless, I opened a daycare first, and tried teaching the kids there how to read, just as I had with my daughter. Guess what happened next? Well, they also learned how to read! That is when I knew I was on to something BIG! I mean I was teaching kids under five years old how to read early, along with doing arithmetic, and some other basic skills. That was all it took for me to write this book. Besides, I have always liked helping others and offering parenting tips, when I found something that really worked or made life easier. That is why I wrote this book --to assist parents in giving their kids a "real" head start in school, by educating their kids early at home.

I also pondered how great it would be if parents everywhere, could give their kids a real head start in school. All they would have to do is make a conscious effort to teach their children how to read ahead of time, along with teaching them some other essential skills. If they could not do it themselves, then maybe they could pay a learning center that specializes in early childhood education to do it for them. I thought if I could start a revolution (major change), and get everyone on board teaching their kids different things early at home; America's kids would definitely get a "real" head start in school.

That is why I *had* to write this book. I wrote it for the children who want to reach their destinies, and for the parents who want to help them reach them. I want all parents everywhere to make a commitment to give their kids a real head start in everything, and it all begins at home. You can do it! I know you can! I believe teaching my kids how to read early and some other things before they started kindergarten, really gave them an advantage in school. You can give your kids this kind of edge in school, too!

So, are you ready to sign up for this movement? This change is necessary, and we *must* do it for our kids. You know something. I have a strong feeling that you are fully on board. Therefore, send me an email at realheadstart@gmail.com to let me know of your commitment to make sure your child receives a quality education. Now that you are on board, continue reading this book for more ideas on how you can give your child a real head start in every grade, and tips on how to keep him/her ahead of the pack.

We have to let our kids know their worth, because we can't expect or wait for teachers to teach our children everything. In the future according to Sally Ride, an American Astronaut, 80% of jobs will require some *background in science and math*, as seen on CNN news. Therefore, if we can start now teaching our kids different things like reading, math, science, and geography at home before they start kindergarten (of course, on their age-level), they'll begin school ready to learn about more things. That means giving them a real head start by teaching them their ABC's, making sure they can recognize their shapes and numbers, and ensuring they understand basic social studies (like who's their Mayor). This also means they should know basic geography (like where in the world do they live), science (like how fruit grows on a tree), and basic punctuation rules, so they can read, write and communicate.

Teachers everywhere are losing their jobs and the numbers of students in classrooms are increasing due to state tax cuts; therefore, we have no other choice but to *teach and work with our children at home, as well as, sending them to school each day.* Let's make sure our kids are learning in school everyday and reviewing what they learn at home. Did you know according to The Atlanta Journal Constitution, recent tax cuts in education have forced schools everywhere to increase their classroom sizes to the state's maximum, allegedly reported in *2. Source: Atlanta Journal Constitution:* http://blogs.ajc.com/get-schooled-blog/2010/05/23/class-size-after-state-board-vote-monday-the-skys-the-limit)? Consequently, over crowded classrooms can make learning difficult for our kids. This is why, more than ever, you must teach and work with your kids at home.

Keep in mind that children are a lot smarter today than we give them credit for, and this is why we can teach our kids how to read and do arithmetic before starting kindergarten. I suppose this is why so many parents are enrolling their children into daycare, whether they work or not. They can see the benefits of enrolling their kids into a daycare that stresses learning, because they want their kids to get a jump-start on acquiring knowledge. Finding a daycare or a learning center that *really teaches* and provides loving care can be hard. I am speaking from experience. I have enrolled my kids in the so-called "learning daycares", and I can assure you that everything my kids knew before I enrolled them in a daycare, they learned at home. I am not bragging, but just making a point that you should do your homework before enrolling your child in the first daycare that claims to offer loving care and "learning". Try enrolling your kids into a Montessori learning center or another daycare that focuses on early education. You may have to interview the center to decide for yourself, if it really focuses on learning and other things, like teaching kids to mind their manners. Ask the parents as they leave the center if their kids are learning and enjoying themselves. They should be able to tell you if their kids are really thriving at the daycare or not. I mean concrete things, like are they learning how to add, subtract, write, read, color, draw, match, and socialize *nicely* with the other children at the center.

I made sure that my children could read, count, add, write, subtract, recite their ABCs and write their address before beginning kindergarten. You can too! If you cannot carve out the time to do it for yourself, that's okay, just pay someone else to do it (...but if you can't afford it right now, make the time to do it for yourself.)! We *must* see to it that our kids get a true head start, by teaching them basic learning skills now at home. If we don't see to it, who will?

Just think about it, each year professors teach students who are prepared for college, right? The students enter college ready to learn on a college level. Therefore, I just think it makes a whole lot of sense that we send our kids to kindergarten ready to learn on a kindergarten level. Teachers cannot do everything, and the last time I checked, they aren't miracle workers, either. So, wouldn't it be great if every child in America were required to know how to read and write before starting kindergarten? This way, our teachers could spend more time teaching our kids other skills that will help them reach their full potentials.

Therefore, encourage your child to listen and pay attention in school, so that he/she can learn what is being taught, in class. I just had a thought. What if every child in America went to school everyday and *really* listened to their teachers, don't you think our kids would naturally learn more? Of course, they would; and, our teachers wouldn't have to use valuable instruction time correcting behavior. Therefore, let's encourage our kids to go to school each day to learn, so that they can grow and broaden their horizons.

Well, China gets it! Watch this YouTube video and see for yourself, a Chinese kindergarten teacher allegedly teaching a group of three and four year olds basic learning skills *early. (3. Source: http://www.youtube.com/watch?v=pUm1j-ScXIs)*

Well, what do you think? Did this video inspire you to start teaching your child some things *early* at home? If these three and four year olds can learn, yours can, too! We do not have to wait until our children turn five to start teaching them how to count or write their ABCs. To be honest, if we wait until our kindergarten teachers teach our kids their ABCs and how to read and write, we could potentially be putting our kids at a disadvantage. Many kids nowadays are beginning kindergarten with reading and writing skills. So, why take a chance on waiting to see what happens? We have to give our kids the best head start we can. Kids do not come out of the womb reading. Therefore, we must take the time to teach our kids how to read ourselves, along with writing and arithmetic.

Every child, in my opinion, is born smart in his or her own way. However, we can make them smarter if we read to them often. We have five years to teach our kids many things, before we are required by law in the United States to enroll them in kindergarten or to start "officially" home schooling them. So, let's take advantage of this time and help our kids learn how to read, write, and do arithmetic before they begin school.

A great learning program to enroll your child into at the age of four is Kumon tm. Go to www.Kumon.com to find out about their admission requirements and the locations in your area. Kumon tm can give your child a head start in school and prepare him/her for success. Although, I highly recommend enrolling your child into Kumon tm, you can teach your child how to read and do basic math at home, yourself. However, if you can afford it, enroll your child today, as well as, continuing to teach him/her different things at home.

Many families in America and in other countries have been helping their kids become smarter for decades. In fact, they are making them so smart, that they're raising the bar for other kids around the world. In many cases, the bar has gotten so high, that some of our kids are finding it hard to reach. As a result, it is literally leaving some of our kids behind. However, we can do something about this. We can also help our kids become smarter and keep them smart. Let's help our kids in everything: sports, music, gymnastics, dance, science, math, computers, writing, etc., because if we don't, it's going to get increasingly harder for our kids to stay in the race, so to speak.

Well, the key to making sure your child receives a quality education is to *start teaching our kids early at home.* This is a lot easier than it sounds. Just keep in mind that kids are born alert, bright, and ready to learn. The difference is what they are exposed to early. Many kindergarten teachers in China are teaching three and four year olds (as referenced in the YouTube video), because they know that very young kids (ages 1-5) can learn many things, if you teach them. Therefore, with this in mind, it is up to us to keep them smart before the world attempts to "dumb them down". If you teach your kids basic learning skills early and keep them ahead, you'll be giving your kids a "real" head start.

Now, let's explore the definition of smart. According to the Webster's dictionary, it means showing intelligence and mental alertness. I know this all too well from watching my children grow up. I watched them learn many things quickly throughout the years from books, educational videos, and music. Here's an interesting story below that will prove to you that kids are born alert, bright, and ready to learn.

When my son was about two days old, he contracted jaundice while he was in the hospital. In any case, he was placed under bili lights with protective glasses to cure him of it. One day, I noticed him peeking from under the small glasses on his face, and I asked the nurse, "Should my baby be peeking from under the glasses?" The nurse replied, "No, the glasses are supposed to be protecting his little eyes from the bili lights, but babies seem to be getting smarter everyday." Then, she secured the glasses with cloth tape, so he couldn't lift them anymore. My point is this. No one told him to use his hand to lift the glasses off his face to take a better look at what was shining down on him. He told his brain to use his hand to lift the glasses, so that he could peek from under the protective eyewear. Although, he didn't know the word for what was on his eyes or a name for whatever was shining down on him, he somehow communicated to his brain to move his hand to the object on his eyes, so he could attempt to look at whatever was shining down on him.

Let's ponder this some more. When you want your hands or legs to do something, don't you have to tell your brain to move them? Of course, you do. We all do it so quickly, that we don't even realize that we told our brains to do anything. Our limbs simply do not move by themselves without being told by our brains to move. Well, there you have it. Babies come into the world with the ability to think and reason. That is why I believe all babies are born smart, and if we teach them things early, as if they are capable of learning, they'll naturally get a head start on acquiring knowledge. Every baby deserves our very best and should have an extraordinary beginning. If we are patient, loving, supportive, and prayerful-- all babies can grow up to be dynamic individuals.

Educating your child at home (in addition to sending him/her to school each day) and encouraging him/her to do his/her best all of the time K-12th grade can be time consuming and exhausting, but worth it. As I mentioned before, both of my kids were reading at the age of three, and I believe that all children can. In my opinion, reading is the key that unlocks the potential that is in every child.

Reading is also the beginning to understanding knowledge or learning new things, whether it is in written or number form.

I've probably said this before, but it's worth repeating. I taught my children how to write their names and the entire alphabet before they started school. In addition, they also learned how to do arithmetic, recognize their colors, and identify shapes, all before beginning kindergarten. If you spend just a few minutes a day teaching your child how to read using the five easy steps in this book, along with some of the other suggestions in this book, I'm confident that your child will begin school with a *real* head start, too!

For those of you with older children, continue working with your kids during the school year, and use the summers to prepare them for the next grade. You'll also find wonderful resources in this book that will help you keep your kids smart and ahead. Whether your kids are starting kindergarten or about to complete the tenth grade, the tips and ideas in this book will help your kids reach their goals.

However, if your child doesn't know how to read yet, you've chosen the right book. This book will inspire you to give your kids a *real* head start in everything, as well as give you reasons why it's imperative (necessary, unavoidable) that you teach your child how to read early. The tips and strategies in this book will assist you in giving your child the best head start possible in school and in all he/she aspires to do.

Teaching our kids how to read "before" they start school is half of the equation to giving our kids a "real" head start. The other half is teaching our children how to write and draw (before starting kindergarten), add and subtract (before starting first grade), multiply and divide (before starting third grade), and so on. This way our kids will start school or each grade prepared to learn and fully participate in classroom discussions. Our kids will also feel sure of themselves and develop a sense of pride in their self-worth. Self-worth means according to Microsoft Dictionary, "confidence in personal value and worth as an individual person and one's belief in oneself". I feel like I need to say what I'm about to say, especially with today's media. We have to teach our teenage boys and teenage girls self-worth, because they have more to offer than their toned physiques, looks, and youthful hair, which I feel today's media put too much emphasis on. Besides, as the good book tells us in Proverbs 31:30, "...charm is deceptive, and beauty is fleeting:", at any rate, let's encourage our kids to get a degree, invent something that will make a difference in others lives, or work on their God-given talents, these are the things that are important and lasting. This is one way we can make sure our "good-looking" kids aren't taken out of class to learn skills their classmates already know. Seeing that when a child is taken out of class to learn how to read or to work on some other skill he/she doesn't know, he/she misses some valuable instruction time in the classroom.

As you can see, reading is the foundation of learning and can make learning a whole lot easier for your child. I believe reading and communication goes hand and hand. Can you imagine sending your child to school without knowing how to read or talk? Of course not, because your child would have a difficult time communicating with his/her teacher and classmates. Think about it for a moment. If your child begins school reading and talking well, he/she will be able to express himself/herself easier, read the chalkboard, read directions on worksheets, and be inspired by all of the positive mottos (sayings) around the classroom. Your child will also be in a position to learn things easier, if he/she goes to school knowing how to read and reason from the start. So, please take some time today to start teaching your child how to read.

Take for instance, my son Joshua excelled in pre-school, kindergarten, first grade, and second grade, while attending Oaks Elementary School in Oaks, Pennsylvania. He is also currently excelling in third grade, at State Bridge Crossing Elementary in Alpharetta, Georgia. My point is this. Joshua excelled in schools up north and is currently excelling in his elementary school down south. For that reason (...in my opinion, and I have seen "Waiting for Superman"), it doesn't matter where your kids attend school, because you can help and encourage them to do their best regardless of what school they attend. I've found that most schools are similar and that the only thing that separates most of them is your child's willingness to learn and do his/her best in school. Therefore, help and encourage your child to do well and learn as much as he/she can, regardless of what school he/she attends.

There are many individuals that like to compare northern and southern schools or private and public schools (none of my readers, I'm sure); nonetheless, I don't subscribe to that kind of thinking, because I believe in the child's ability and motivation to learn, not the school's reputation, whether it's good or bad. Because some of our kids don't get to decide, where they will live or go to school, and the last time I checked most of them don't pay to attend private school, either. Therefore, it isn't fair to judge our kids on the schools they attend; however, what we can do is make sure that they learn what is being taught in class, regardless of where they attend.

Simply put, I taught Joshua how to read, write, communicate, and to do arithmetic all before he started kindergarten. When Joshua was in kindergarten, first, and second grade I worked with him during the school year and during the summers. I made sure he did all of his homework assignments neatly and correctly. I checked every homework problem, and when he didn't understand something, I took the time to explain it to him. I made sure he was prepared for tests and quizzes. I also encouraged him to read and learn extra skills at home. Well, he is in third grade this year (doing very well) and I'm still working with him at home, and you can do this with your child, too. Just follow my example above.

I've also had the opportunity to watch Chelsea, our daughter, excel in kindergarten through eighth grade (there were a few bumps in ninth grade, but she made it through nicely). She recently, made all A's and B's on her tenth grade report card dated 1/20/2011(Whew!). Your kids can and will do well in school, too, if you work with them at home and encourage them to do their best. One way to do this is to know what grades your child are making at school, and to make sure he/she is listening and following school rules. To accomplish this, just ask your child's teacher for a progress report every four weeks that shows your child's grades and behavior, this way you can help and encourage him/her to do better in class (if he/she needs it.). Nevertheless, all it takes is a little planning and some executing (implementing) on your part to help your child succeed in and out of the classroom.

Remember kids respect what you inspect. In other words, look over your kids work to make sure that they are prepared for their quizzes and tests. If you do this, your kids will be motivated to study a little harder if they know that you are going to quiz them before every quiz and test. I've used this technique with both of my kids, and they both pay more attention in class now. If they don't know what they are expected to know for the quiz or the test, then back to the drawing board. What kid wants to do that? That is why my kids are prepared the first time, so that they'll have some "me" time. So, do this with your kids, and they'll be ready for all of their tests and quizzes.

The summer is the perfect time to teach your kids new skills for the upcoming school year. I have spent many summers preparing my kids for the next grade, and so can you! Every year, I just make it a commitment to get my kids ready for the next school year. I hope I'm convincing you to work with your kids over the summer, too. You can be your child's tutor over the summer, or you can enroll them in learning centers like Kumon™ and Sylvan™. Don't forget to have your kids work on the websites mentioned in the back of this book, over the summer, as well.

Simply put, the tips found in this book are easy to follow and implement into your child's schedule. This book will also encourage you to continue working with your children through 12th grade, because according to research done by the NCES *(4. National Center for Education Standards in 2007)*, 26% of eighth graders cannot read at a basic level. That's disappointing, especially when we think our kids are learning valuable instruction at school each day. Let's face it, just as we expect "all" nurses to do their jobs well (because we never know which one we are going to get during a check up), we expect "all" teachers to do their jobs well, too. In today's world, our kids need caring and attentive teachers, but we must also encourage our kids to read to become better readers. I'm fortunate that my kids have had and still have wonderful teachers, which are caring and very competent. Nevertheless, we can't sit back and just hope that our kids are learning in school. You have to work with your kids at home, as well as work with their teachers, so that your kids will be reading and learning on their grade levels. If you feel like your child isn't learning something or not quite getting a concept that is being or has been taught in

13

class, don't hesitate to ask your child's teacher for help. Most teachers welcome parent involvement and questions. Don't be embarrassed to admit that you can't help your child with a certain subject, instead get your child some help from a tutor or his/her teacher. Now, this is something every parent in America can do!

In my opinion, we're in a war. We are not at war in the traditional sense, but at war, just the same. We can no longer sit back and watch while some of our kids are being left behind. We must go to bat for our kids, by working with them at home and seeing to it that they get a quality education. We have to, if we want our kids to have a real chance at achieving the American dream (to have success and prosperity according to *47. http://en.wikipedia.org/wiki/ American_Dream*), and achieving more than we did.

CHAPTER II

On Making the Commitment

Well, the first thing I'm going to suggest is for you to make a commitment that you're going to spend quality time helping your child become a little smarter each day. As I mentioned before, all children are brilliant. Our job is to merely build on this brilliance and keep them that way. It is our duty as parents to make sure that our kids become productive citizens one day. The second thing I'm going to suggest is that you give your child piano, violin, or guitar lessons and encourage him/her to practice at least fifteen minutes a day (It is better to practice a little each day, than to skip a whole lot of days doing nothing.). This will not be easy, because some kids will push back (or wait for you to tell them to practice), but it's worth it. The third thing I am going to recommend is that you enroll your child into a sport program like peewee soccer, gymnastics, track or little league basketball. I noticed that when my kids started participating in sports, they automatically became more competitive, not only in sports but in every area of their lives. Competition is a great motivator, and it can encourage your child to work harder at all he/she does. Competition can also inspire your child to be a winner at school, at home, at sports, and at everything, he/she does!

You should really focus on enrolling your child in sports, because according to *40. http://www.ehow.com/ facts 5183402 do-sports-kids .html* studies show that children who are involved in sports naturally do their best at everything. Another important benefit is that you are incorporating physical fitness into your child's daily routine, and that's always a plus. I have found that children who participate in sports are often more confident and do better in school (it's like their minds are clearer and they are less fidgety). Any physical exercise, whether it's from participating in sports or from playing outside everyday can help your child release endorphins, which are great stress busters. Nevertheless, in my opinion, my kids are more self-assured and focused because of sports, and I'm convinced that your kids will be too.

According to *41.* http://musiced.about.com/od/ beginnersguide/a/pinst.htm schoolchildren who play at least one musical instrument appears smarter, do better in school, and perform well on standardized tests. I strongly believe that *children who are involved in music and in sports are just more disciplined, competitive, and confident.* The fourth thing I am going to suggest is that you feed your child lots of fruits and vegetables, lean meats, beans, nuts and whole grain breads and carbohydrates, like brown rice and whole-wheat pasta. I strongly believe that "a well nourished child flourishes at everything." The fifth thing I am going to suggest is that you give your child a lot of praise as he/she learns to read and do new things. This kind of praise and encouragement will do wonders for your child's self-esteem. Finally, the sixth thing I'm going to suggest is for you to take your child to museums, plays, and to the library, which is always free and a favorite of mine. In addition, make sure your child gets plenty of rest, as you work with him/her during the school year to keep him/her ahead.

If you can, it is always a good idea to expose your kids to new math and science skills, before they learn about them in school. There is computer software available today that can help you give your kids a head start in math and science. Try the Southwestern School Sets at http://www.southwesternathome.com/southwestern-company-products.aspx?p=27. It's learning software from Southwestern that focuses on giving your kids a head start in school. In addition, work with your kids regularly, so that they will retain what they learn in school and acquire new skills that will give them an advantage in school. In my opinion, it is better to keep your kids ahead, then for them to play catch up. Just focus on giving your kids a head start before every new grade, and I'm certain that they'll succeed that school year. Make sure your kids are always learning something new. This will help your child achieve his/her scholastic goals in school, as well as, prepare for his/her future.

Another thing, it is important to make learning fun! One way to accomplish this goal is to play games like Scrabble tm, Monopoly tm, Chess tm, The Game of LIFE tm, Family Feud tm, Jeopardy tm, Who Wants to Be a Millionaire tm, and Are You Smarter than a Fifth Grader? tm with your kids. Games like these will help your kids practice math, reading, and encourage good old-fashioned thinking. Your kids will be having so much fun that they won't even realize they're learning anything at all. As you can see, you do not have to spend a whole lot of money to keep your kids smart. Your time, energy, and attentiveness to your kids' education can do wonders, and it will definitely keep them in the race (so to speak)--comfortably. Therefore, follow the steps and advice in this book and you'll see your kids transform right before your eyes.

Joshua's teachers are always amazed at how prepared he is for school each year, after a long summer break. If you use my techniques over the summer, your child's teachers will be astonished, too. The tips in this book, if implemented, will give your child a head start that will sustain him/her throughout the school year. Nevertheless, continue working with your child to keep him/her ahead. You may get some push back if your child is in grades 8th-12th, but again, it's worth it.

Now, that I've mentioned this age group (13-18 years old), here are a few suggestions that will keep your teenagers on task. Tell your teenagers to hand over the cell phone and/or the iPod as soon as they arrive home from school each day, so they can concentrate on doing their homework. You may give the cell phone and the iPod back to them after all of the homework is done, but it's also a good idea to get both of them back before your kids go to bed. Why? Well, just in case you didn't know, some schoolchildren (right around the 7th and 8th grade--and for some sooner) will fall asleep with iPods in their ears and talk on the phone until 2:00 am in the morning, on a school night. Don't be naïve when it comes to your teenagers. I'm speaking from experience, and I've had a few wake up calls concerning this topic myself, so I should know. So, *stay alert* and committed in helping your child stay focused during the school year, because our kids can make good grades in school, we just need to make sure that they do all of their schoolwork and chapter reading. Please don't think that *your child* won't be *tempted* to talk on the phone late on a school night or listen to music into the wee hours of the morning, because our kids are children, not saints. In addition, you shouldn't allow your kids to have televisions with cable and computers in their rooms, either. It's a bad idea, but if you think it isn't a bad idea, at least protect your child's innocence and turn on all the parental blocks on your child's computer and television. You must set expectations in your home, that there will be no video or computer time (unless he/she needs it to work on one of the websites mentioned in this book or to do his/her homework) until all homework is done. This is just a suggestion, but whatever you do, you must have rules around using the cell phone, iPod, Wii (and other video game systems), Facebook, Twitter, and Myspace (not to mention other social networking media sites). These digital devices and websites can be distractions, and we must help our kids manage their time around them wisely.

Another thing you can do to keep the older and younger schoolchildren on task is to follow their grades on real time website services like Parent Connect, Skyward, or whatever online grade tracker your child's school uses. If your child's school doesn't offer a grade tracker, just ask the teacher how your child is doing in school on a regular basis. This way, if your child is performing below his/her standard, you can get him/her some help or help him/her yourself. As mentioned before, kids respect what you inspect.

We can't just talk about our kids getting a quality education; we have to insist that our kids are learning on their grade levels. We have to help them do well in their current grades, as well as, get them ready for the next grade. If we can work with our kids during the school year and over summer breaks, starting in kindergarten, our kids will do well in school every year. This will ultimately lead to them graduating from high school, and hopefully going off to college to acquire more skills before entering the workforce or starting their own businesses or careers.

You probably are thinking, "Gee, when do the poor kids get a break?" My kids get time off, but I don't want their brains to go on vacation, too. That is why I make sure they learn, read, and review over the summer. You should do this for your kids, also. Believe me, I am not the only parent who is focusing on their child's education over the summer. Many kids in America are tutored in libraries throughout the summer. Why should you care? Well, all of us should care, because these are the very students our kids will be competing against in the future. These same kids will attend school in the fall ready to learn, and their teachers will be delighted to teach them on their levels. I believe this is how the bar is raised, and if we aren't helping our kids to stay competitive, they can potentially be left behind. The question is, "Will your child be ready for the next grade?" The kids that work on skills over the summer, isn't necessarily smarter than your child, they are just more prepared to learn in the fall. If you cannot afford a tutor to work with your child over the summer, tutor your child yourself. You should also encourage your child to work on the websites mentioned in the back of this book over the summer, to give your child a jump-start on the coming school year.

Before I go any further, I want you to know that I will stress certain points repeatedly throughout this book, to emphasize the importance of giving your child the best head start you can in school, sports, music, dance, and more! I really want parents to help their kids reach their goals and help them to share their God given talents and brains with the world.

Now, back to if my kids get a break during the summer. Sure, they do! My kids have lots of fun during the summer. They travel, attend camps and concerts, go skating, bowling, swimming, and to the movies, visit amusement parks and museums, dine at restaurants (which is always fun!), and so much more! Nonetheless, I try to encourage them to *read*, play the piano, and practice Spanish (or Latin) over the summer months, too. I also give them math and reading worksheets from www.edhelper.com to complete and whatever else I can think of that would help prepare them for the upcoming school year. Nevertheless, they are prepared for school in the fall.

Working with your kids over the summer or making sure, they sign up with Kumon™ or Sylvan™ is just a practical thing to do. All it takes is a little scheduling and a whole lot of cooperation from your kids. You have to make kids accountable for their own accomplishments; by making sure, they respect their teachers and study hard in school. One way to do this is to make a game out of it, by rewarding them with _____ (you fill in the blank) if they do their best in school each marking period.

You should also reward your kids for reading, because children, who read, learn a lot. How can you get your kids to read more *and* enjoy it? Well, you might start by challenging them to a reading marathon and rewarding them for every ten books or short stories they read. For an example, some of your prizes might be an iTunes card, a pair of shoes (you know-- the ones that cost a lot of money), a DVD, favorite team jersey, video game or some money to spend at the mall. You probably were going to buy these things anyway, so why not make your kids earn them. It does not really matter what the rewards are, as long as you're encouraging your kids to read more. Next, take it up a few notches and reward them for learning a different language like Spanish or French, for learning how to play a musical instrument, or for volunteering in the line of work they want to go into in the future. The rewards should reflect the difficulty of the tasks accomplished.

The important thing to remember is that you are making learning fun and rewarding for your kids. By rewarding your kids, they will naturally want to read more, and consequently, learn more. Now, when your kids go back to school in the fall, their teachers are going to be so amazed at how prepared your kids are to learn!

We all hear the compliment, especially during or after summer vacation, "Wow, the kids have grown so much!" It's great for people to say that our kids have grown over the summer, but it's even better when they are complimenting you on how smart or talented your child is or how he/she carries himself/herself. It's a reminder that you're doing something right, and to keep working with your child at home.

It's also easier for our teachers, when students return to school in the fall ready to learn. Just think about it, if every parent and every business made education a priority. Our kids would be motivated to do their best in school *everyday*. How can we do this? I know one way, by rewarding kids for doing well in school, and this can begin right in our own homes. Everyone must get involved and have high expectations for our kids. We all can motivate America's kids to do their best. All we have to do is change the dialogue, instead of asking them about frivolous (trivia) things, ask them how they are doing in school, sports, music, or in other activities. I believe this can motivate our kids to do well in school and in extra-curricular activities, because it will send a message that being smart and doing great things, are the things that are respected. For starters, if we could get the entire community, teachers, parents, and grandparents doing something special for our kids when they make all A's and B's, this would make a BIG difference in our kids' attitude about learning. We all can do something to help the children in America get smarter, so let's do it!

Did you know according to *28.* http://www.infoplease.com/ipa/A0923110.html about 250,000 15 year olds in

41 countries participated in a math, science, and reading skills assessment? Well, the findings were mind-boggling! They found that America (that would be us) is *number 25 in math, number 12 in reading, and number 20 in science* around the world. Really? Unbelievable! This couldn't be true about America's kids, right? Well, it is. I hope these findings encourage every American to work with their kids at home. We have to help our children get smarter. We have to improve America's standings in math, science, and reading by helping our kids get a quality education. I told you we were in a war, not a real war as I mentioned before, but sort of like an "education war". Instead of who is the fittest, it's coming down to who is the smartest. We have to encourage America's kids to step up. Our kids can do better in science, math, and reading, and they must be held accountable for their own grades and behavior in school. They must go to school to learn each day, not to play and give their peers and teachers a hard time.

Just think about it. People work everyday and are paid to perform a certain task or service "well", right? No one wants to pay for or respects an okay job. All I'm suggesting is that we expect the same from our kids and reward them for doing "well" in school, sports, music, and in whatever they do. So, what can parents do to help? Well, parents can work (teach and review) with their kids at home and reward them for doing their best in everything they do. Here is a quote I saw on the back of a Parkview High School athlete's shirt in Lilburn, Georgia the other day that is worth mentioning to your child when you feel he/she hasn't given his/her best in a game, on a report card, or in a competition -- "If you don't invest very much, then defeat doesn't hurt very much, and winning isn't very exciting." Here is another one worth quoting when your child needs a little reminding to not become complacent with just doing an okay job-- "…we are going to relentlessly chase perfection, knowing well we will not catch it, because nothing is perfect. But we are going to relentlessly catch it, because in the process we will catch excellence." Vince Lombardi.

It will probably be hard at first, but make your kids earn special outings and extra things instead of just giving it to them. For an example, if your child makes an A or B on a test, you can take them to that museum they wanted to visit or you can make their favorite meal for dinner or give them a $25 Visa gift card (which is always a winner). Anyway, it doesn't matter so much, what the reward is, as long as it motivates them to keep doing well in school. How can businesses help? Businesses can reward our children who make all A's and B's with a gift card, a free kid's meal, admission to a popular amusement park, a Barnes & Nobel gift card, a DVD, a video game or toy. Businesses should encourage patrons to donate toys, gift cards, or similar items throughout the school year to give to children who perform well on their report cards. Businesses should also put up posters that will remind schoolchildren in grades K-12 to do their best in school and to bring in their all A's and all A's and B's report cards for a prize. I know it sounds like something out of a movie, but all of this can be done. We have to get out and make it happen, because it is certainly in our power to do so. If we can show our kids that education is important and not just talk about it, maybe our children will be motivated to graduate from high school on time and go off to college.

With all the talk these days, about making sure our kids are not left behind. I started thinking about the "No Child Left Behind" initiative. It was designed to make sure that children received a high-quality education, so that they wouldn't be left behind. The irony is that the students were being "left behind" if they didn't meet all the requirements.

I am concerned that this initiative may just be doing more harm than good, because it is not uncommon to hear about seventeen year olds in ninth grade. If these kids fail to pass the class a second time, they could find themselves in the same grade the following year, and become discouraged. Some of these kids eventually drop out of school, and this is exactly what we don't want to happen. I know we don't want to believe this can happen, but I believe this is why some of America's kids aren't graduating from high school or not graduating on time. Some of our kids are even dropping out of school at alarming rates. Therefore, it makes me think that the "No Child Left Behind" initiative, although it intentions were good at first, has turned into an obstacle for some of our children. Anyhow, this is why we have to work with our kids at home. We have to make sure that our kids are paying attention in class, so that they *can* do well in school.

We also have counselors at school and other support staff that could help. That is why I cannot understand why so many of our children are failing, not graduating on time, and dropping out of school. Counselors should have some idea how every child assigned to them is doing in school. This way they can help the students who aren't doing so well, before it is too late to do anything about it. If the counselor's computer can some how alert him/her of any or all students who aren't making at least a B in class, he/she could then make the necessary steps to help the student or students turn things around. The bottom line is that everyone is responsible here, including the students. Besides, counselors don't know what they don't know. Perhaps teachers could notify counselors of the students who aren't making at least a B in their classes-- while there is still time to do something about it. Then, the counselors could encourage these students to listen more in class or find out what is going on in their lives that may be distracting them. Counselors could also meet with parents and come up with study plans to help their kids get back on track, as well.

Again, we must work with our kids during the summer, because it is the perfect opportunity to teach our kids fresh ideas and help them review and get a jump-start on the upcoming school year. It is also a wonderful time to take them to libraries, museums, theatres, and aquariums to open their minds to new concepts and viewpoints. If you do this for your child, you will make it easier for him/her to expand on knowledge he/she already knows.

In addition, I think kids learn and retain information better if they are taught lessons frequently. It doesn't matter if children are learning how to do division or how to identify shapes. If they review the lesson often, they will start to remember it. It just makes a lot of sense to me. When a child is introduced to a skill or a fact before he/she learns it in school, and practices it often, he/she will retain it. Think of it in this way. Do you agree that children learn best in layers, one brick at a time? I think so, because Rome wasn't built in a day, and our kids won't learn everything in a day, either.

Your child should learn all of his "firsts" at home, because you are his/her "first" teacher. One of the first things you should teach your child to do is learn how to read. Teaching your child how to read consist of five easy steps that can be found in this book. Your child will review and learn something new each step. You will also be encouraged to teach your child how to count, add, write, subtract, along with some other things. No, you don't need a teaching degree (smile) to teach your child these things, just a desire to give him/her a real head start in school.

Think about it for a moment. Why do you think teachers ask questions like this one, "Who can tell me what a haiku is?" To be honest I really don't know why they ask things they haven't taught yet, but the student who answers the question correctly has probably learned it at home or some place else. He/She also could have learned it from a book, during the previous school year, over the summer, or at a museum. Therefore, the point I am trying to make is that the child who does answer the question right feels good about himself/herself. His/Her confidence naturally soars. Yes, just like that, he/she builds assurance in his/her ability to learn and retain information. His/Her teacher and classmates will also begin to respect him/her for being so clever. This positive attention can make a child feel good about himself/herself and encourage him/her to learn more. All of these things have to stand for something. If your child is encouraged and praised for being smart or for being able to do something extraordinary, he'll/she'll continue to learn and excel in school. This is a critical point to remember and to put into practice.

You probably are thinking, "Do I continue working with my child after he/she begins kindergarten?" Absolutely. You should continue working with your child all the way through 12th grade! You will be helping him/her keep the *real* head start you gave him/her in the first place. So, you can't give up now. You only have to do this for another 12 years. Nevertheless, God bless the parents who have to work with their kids in college, too! Of course, you will want to encourage your child while he/she is in college, but you shouldn't have to be so hands on as you were in grades K-12th. Remember, you'll be one of your child's biggest supporters, second to God. Therefore, let's help our teachers teach our children by working with our kids at home. All you have to do is make sure your child does his/her homework everyday, and remind him/her to be respectful to his/her teachers, and to listen and pay attention in class. In addition, don't forget to encourage your child to read throughout the school year and during the summers.

One awesome website to try for reading, math, science, and writing practice is www.edhelper.com . Your child can use this website to work on his/her math and reading skills. It is also a great website to read and learn about past presidents, famous people, and inventors. Another great website to try for math is www.ixl.com. It's really a terrific website to have your child practice his/her math skills.

Before I forget, I've found it's a good idea to have younger children practice their writing, drawing, and communication skills by writing a story about something that happened at school each week. You might want to have your child do this activity at least twice a week. Also, supply your child with markers, crayons, glitter, and glue to encourage him/her to make his/her drawings nicer. Another way to give your child a real head start is to introduce him/her to a foreign language using Rosetta Stone software or some other language software. I promise you, if you continue to be involved in your child's education as President Barack Obama's mother did (it obviously helped President Barack Obama a lot), you'll begin to see a difference in your child's confidence, grades, and standardized tests.

Remember, it doesn't matter what your background is, what color you are, or how much money you make, or where you live; I believe you have it in you to make sure your child gets a quality education. Your child can learn many things if you are willing to work with him/her on a daily basis, and trust me this isn't always easy. When you are trying to juggle a job, your family, friends, church, and other interests, working with your child *also* can easily be put on the back burner. Nevertheless, it can be exciting and rewarding getting your child ready for kindergarten or for the next grade. If you missed getting your child prepared for kindergarten, that's okay, just do it for the other grades, and continue working with him/her throughout the school year, too.

Keep in mind; it's never too late to work with your child. You can boost your child's education from kindergarten through 12th grade, just by supplementing his/her schoolwork with extra work at home. It's all about the resources and educational experiences you give to your child. Another thing to remember, as I have mentioned before, is that you don't have to wait for teachers or anyone else to teach your child how to read or to do anything. You can do it yourself.

You have five years to work with your child before they are "required by law" to enter school or be home-schooled. Take advantage of this time, because before you know it, your local school will be contacting you to test your child for kindergarten. Here's something to consider. I believe kindergartners are placed with other students who are learning at or near their school readiness. Again, this is my opinion. Nevertheless, you should give your child the best head start you can give him/her by teaching him/her how to read, write, do arithmetic, draw, and identify shapes before he/she starts kindergarten.

Remember to remind your child *each day* to listen in class and to be respectful to all his/her teachers and classmates. Could you imagine teaching in a classroom all day, where you had to ask students to be quiet all day long? Well, that is exactly what is happening in many classrooms today. That is why it is so important to talk to our kids about behaving in school, so that their teachers can teach them more effectively. If good behavior in school were being reinforced at home, kids would naturally act better at school and learn more. Therefore, mom and dad, remind your kids to behave in school, so that they'll do better in class.

How can we get America's kids to behave in school? Well, sometimes the change we want to see in America's kids, have to begin with our own kids. I'm sure our kids don't need to be corrected, but just to be on the safe side, let's remind them to behave in school, anyway. Also, while I'm thinking about it, let's encourage our kids to treat their classmates and every child at school the way they want to be treated. In other words, let's encourage our kids to be leaders, not bullies.

Parents, we must tell our children to behave in class, to listen when the teacher is instructing, to stay in their seats, and to keep their hands to themselves, so that they will receive a quality education.

Therefore, parents, we are in this together. Do we really want teachers going over lessons quickly, just to check it off their lists, because they didn't get the time to teach it the way they had planned to? We have to realize that each school year builds on the other, and remind our kids to behave in school. If your child does not learn all of the requirements for this year's math class, for instance, next year's math teacher will just assume that your child is ready to build on what he/she has learned last year. This is when your child could potentially become discouraged and fall further behind. It is not fair to our kids when they can't learn in school, because the teacher has to stop and correct the students who are misbehaving in class; nor is it fair to our teachers. Therefore, we must remind and insist that our kids respect their teachers and listen in class.

I know from personal experience how difficult it is for teachers to discipline students who just won't listen and cooperate. I remember my twelfth grade English teacher, who tried diligently to teach us everyday, but had a difficult time doing so. She had a hard time, because there were students in the back of the classroom (which reminds me, make sure your kids sit up front in class) constantly interrupting her. Their disruptions made it impossible for her to teach the class the way she wanted to. When kids act out at school, not only are they preventing themselves from learning, but they are also making it difficult for their peers to learn, too. So, let me tell you the rest of my story. I felt very sorry for my 12th grade English teacher during my last year in high school. She was gentle and extremely soft-spoken. I didn't realize it at the time (because I was excited about starting Florida State University in the fall), but my teacher and the students in the class (including me) was being affected by the unruly students in the back of the room. Memories like this one *can become rare*, if parents everywhere would just take a few moments everyday to remind their kids to behave in school each day. Therefore, let's do our part and remind our kids to behave in class each day, because we wouldn't want the teacher to stop the class to correct our child's behavior, now would we?

That is why it's so important to work with our children at home each day, because to be honest you don't know which day your child's teacher won't get to teach as much as she/he had planned to teach that day. If the teacher has to stop often to correct disruptive students in class, who knows how much she'll/he'll actually get to teach. Therefore, ask your kids about their school day over dinner, to see what is happening at school, and take this opportunity to remind him/her to respect and listen to his/her teacher.

After reading this book, your child should be one of the kids in class that is contributing positively, and not among the students in class who are choosing to be out of control. In other words, your child should be a part of the solution, not part of the problem.

If your child is doing well in school, great; however, if he/she isn't continue working with him/her until he/she does. On the other hand, if your child isn't doing as well in school as you know he/she is capable of doing, start looking for distracters right away. Now, that you have found those diverters, help your child focus more on his/her schoolwork, by limiting his/her use of these diverters.

Here are more suggestions on how to keep your kids on track. Take the time to make sure they complete all of their homework, along with doing worksheets and working on some of the websites in this book. The reason I'm telling you to give your kids some extra schoolwork at home, is to keep them ahead. If you can, try spending at least 30 minutes a day teaching your kids something new or reviewing something with them. The important thing here is to stay involved in your kids' education and stay supportive and consistent. Whatever you do, never give up on your kids. You must always motivate your kids to do their best in school. Who knows, one of your kids might just become a famous talk show host, like Oprah Winfrey someday?

Think about this for a moment. Ask any child in the world what they want to be when they grow up, and you'll never get responses like these: "When I grow up, I want to be homeless.", "When I grow up, I am going to drop out of school.", or "When I grow up, I am *not* going to college." Nevertheless, these unfortunate scenarios happen for some everyday. Even so, it doesn't have to happen if we give our kids a real head start in everything. So, remember to teach your kids not to steal, lie, cheat, or hurt anyone. Remind them to treat others the way they'd like to be treated. More importantly, I hope pointing out that no one wants to grow up and have a dismal existence, has encouraged you to work with your child at home. I hope it has inspired you to teach your child to respect others, as well as himself/herself. I hope I've motivated you to teach your child to obey the rules at school and in life. I promise you that if you use the suggestions, tips, examples, and steps in this book your child will soar like an eagle and reach his/her goals. So, start working and talking with your child today, because I know you want your child's dreams to come true.

Remember, as your child's parent, you have a tremendous opportunity here to intervene early in your child's education before he/she begins school. We all can give our kids an awesome head start before they begin school, because we all can use the websites in this book to teach our kids different things. You don't have to enroll your child in a private daycare either, to give him/her a great head start in school. All you have to do is have a true desire to give your child the best head start in school. One-way to do this is to read to your child as much as you can, as well as, encourage him/her to read on his/her own, too (if he/she is reading already). Have your child read to you sometimes, if he/she can, regardless of how old he/she is. Feel free to correct your child if he/she pronounces a word wrong. If you both aren't sure how to pronounce a word, go to the following website, www.merriam-webster.com, enter the word, and click on the speaker icon for the correct pronunciation.

Once again, thank you for purchasing this book, and I personally wish you the best of luck on teaching your child how to read and on giving him a "real" head start in school and in life.

Remember, once you're committed to helping your child receive the best education possible, yes, you can help him/her do well in school. Don't take the chance that your child will be the one who won't learn to read in kindergarten or learn some other basic skill. Therefore, make sure you teach your child how to read at home, along with some other basic skills *before* your child starts school.

CHAPTER III

Yes You CAN Teach Your Child How To Read Early and More!

Yes, you CAN teach your child how to read early, and so much more! The more children learn, the more they will know, and the more they know, the more they will accomplish. That is why I am encouraging you to teach and introduce your child to as much knowledge as you can. "Give Our Kids A Real Head Start", is going to encourage you to teach your kids how to read early, as well as, teach them some other basic learning skills. It is also filled with all kinds of wonderful and fun tips on how to teach a child how to read *and* give him/her a real head start in every grade.

When I decided to write this book a while back, I thought to myself, "What would I share?" Do I have enough to say about giving kids a real head start in school for a whole book? Where do I begin? Will my readers experience the same kind of success I did? How will I get my book into their hands? Then, it dawned on me to stop thinking about everything and just write the book. So, I decided to just share my heart and talk to my readers, as if you were in front of me. I hope you are enjoying this book so far, and learning different ways you can assist your child in school. Thanks again for purchasing this book, and I hope this book is a blessing to you and your child.

Well, regardless of how things are going right now, it's about to get a whole lot better. When you take on a project like giving your child a real head start in school and teaching him/her how to read early, it can be challenging but so rewarding. So, sit back and enjoy while you read and learn more tips that will help you give your child the head start every parent dreams of today. You are about to go on a journey that will help and inspire you to teach your child how to read and more! Who knows, you may even learn something in the process. I know I did!

Well, first I want you to know that you are going to be successful at teaching your child how to read, along with teaching him/her some other things. This book has everything you need to help your child learn to read and many tips to give your child an excellent head start in school, sports, music, and almost anything you can think of that can help your child grow. Well, let's get started. Remember, the overall mission here is to teach your child how to read early, and to give him/her a real head start in every grade and keep him/her ahead.

Well, here's my story and all you have to do is tweak (adjust) it here and there to make it work for you and your child. For an example, if your child is going to first or second grade and cannot read yet, that's okay. I am confident that he/she will be reading in no time. Just keep implementing the steps in this book, and you'll get the results you're seeking for your child. If your child knows how to sing the alphabet song and can recognize and say each letter, skip step one and proceed to step two. Your child should know how to sing the ABCs, say each letter and know the sound of each letter before moving on to step three.

One sure way to teach your child how to read is to read to him/her everyday. I believe the key to teaching your child anything is persistence and repetition. You must be willing to invest a lot of time and energy to teach your child how to read, along with some other skills.

With this in mind, let me finish my story. It all started when I found out, I was pregnant with my first baby, *Chelsea*. I was so excited! I read every book I could get my hands on about babies. I watched every television program and listened to all kinds of stories about babies long ago. I guess somewhere along the way, I got this idea to read to my baby, although, she wasn't born, yet. You see, I was a little over seven and a half months pregnant and full of anticipation when I got this wonderful idea to read to my baby. For a brief moment, I thought how silly it is to be reading to a baby that wasn't even born yet. However, I knew my baby could hear sounds in the womb, because I read somewhere that babies could hear in the womb. So, I decided to ignore how silly it seemed and I read to my baby anyway.

Let me paint a picture for you. The nursery was ready and pretty in pink. My check-ups were going great. My baby shower was in about a month, and to be honest there was nothing else to do but read to my baby. Ultimately, that is just what I decided to do, read to my baby. My due date was approximately one month and some weeks away, and I could feel my baby moving every time I read to her (I guess she was enjoying it!). As a result, I felt like I was doing something good for my baby, and it just felt right. You can begin reading to your child right now, whether you are pregnant or not. You can begin reading to your child at any age, and it doesn't matter if your child is a month old, three years old, seven years old, or 15 years old (Yes, you can read *with* this age group. Try reading the classics or a few plays together. That's always fun!). What matters is that you are reading to or with your child, and that he/she is learning different things. It is never too soon or too late to introduce your child to reading. Don't worry a whole lot about what books to read, just read to or with your child. You can visit your local bookstore or library today and choose a few books to read. By the way, The Golden Classic collection is always a great selection to choose for the younger children.

Even if I had never read it anywhere, I would have believed that baby Chelsea (Yes, my husband and I had already picked out a name for our little girl.) was listening to me read, when I was pregnant with her. The fact that she would move every time I read to her, proved to me that she could hear everything. So, just like that I reasoned that if she could hear me read, then she could hear music, if I played it. That is when I started playing classical music, and I continued this routine of reading and playing classical music up until the day she was born. After she was born, you guessed it, I continued reading and playing classical music for my beautiful baby.

Well, as Chelsea grew, I would sit her in my lap and read to her all the time. As I read to her, I would point to pictures, words, colors, and some of the characters and asked her questions about them. Although she was not talking yet, it was fun to watch her point and look at all of the pictures in the book when she was around 13 months old. I would ask her questions just for the fun of it. I never expected any real answers, although she answered me every time or pointed to the correct pictures. Well, at least I wanted to believe this is what she was doing. You know how we parents are; we *all* think our babies are the smartest and the prettiest. Well, that's exactly what I was thinking about Chelsea, at 15 months old. I was thinking how blessed I am to have such a pretty and smart baby girl. (Who hasn't done this?)

She also loved listening to classical music and other nursery songs at naptime. Consequently, I took advantage of my baby's love for music, and played nursery songs that went over numbers, colors, and the alphabet. It was just a lot of fun to watch her grow smarter everyday. I also talked and sung to her all the time. It did not matter if I was giving her a bath or making her a bottle, I was always talking to her as if she understood me. I sung songs she listened to at naptime like: the alphabet song, the number song, and the color song. As I mentioned before, it helps when your child hears something repeatedly. For instance, singing the alphabet song and other nursery songs with or to your child regularly can help him/her learn it without much effort. It's hard to believe, but your child is already learning part of step one, which is learning how to sing the alphabet song. Your child will also learn how to recognize the letters of the alphabet in step one. The first two reading steps are easy, but shouldn't be rushed. Keep in mind that some kids may learn to sing the alphabet song quicker than expected, but on the other hand, some may take a little longer than expected. The important thing to remember is that every child learns at his or her own pace. Just remain patient with your child and encourage him/her while he/she learns each step. Learning how to read is a process that must be learned one-step at a time. Another thing I enjoyed doing when Chelsea was a baby, was to play children's CDs in the car for her, as I ran errands. The CDs entertained her and taught her indirectly how to count and sing her ABCs. When she was old enough to sing along, we sung the songs together at home and in the car. She enjoyed it a great deal! If you do not want to sing the songs along with your baby (because you feel silly and a little uncomfortable), then encourage your baby to sing them to you.

Talk to your kids while you run errands, because they are paying more attention than we think they are. For instance, when Chelsea was about two years old, she would point to and name all the different fruits and vegetables in the produce department at the grocery store. I was thrilled and almost couldn't believe how smart and vocal she was. I am sharing these important milestones with you to prove that talking to your baby works and you should do it with your child, too, to get the same results I got with my kids. It's imperative that you communicate to your baby everyday and it doesn't matter how young your baby is. Just talk to your baby the way you want him/her to talk to you one day. Of course, it's okay to talk *sweetly* to your baby, but try not to talk gibberish (nonsense talk) all the time. You wouldn't want your baby to mistake "gibberish" for the family's language, would you? You probably are thinking, "What do I say to a baby that can't talk yet or understand anything I'm saying?" You can say many things to your baby. From day one you can say, "Hello, sweet baby." You can also tell him/her what you are doing. For an example, if you are about to change your baby's diaper, you can say, "Mommy's getting ready to change your diaper". Well, I think you get the idea. I believe my kids started reading early, because not only did I introduce them to the *written word* early, I also communicated the *spoken word* to them. The important thing is that you are talking with your baby. Furthermore, use a lot of inflection (tone of voice, happy, and upbeat) when you talk to your baby. Pets listen to our tones when we talk to them, and babies listen to our tone of voices, too.

Read to your child the way you would want him to read to you someday. Your baby is learning how to talk and read everyday from you, so remember to make the best impression you can. Every interaction and every book you read to your baby are the components needed to help your baby talk and read someday. It's also important to keep your child interested in every story you read by asking him/her questions. For an example, if the book says, "Sammy wants the blue ball." You can say, "Where is the blue ball?" Obviously, you want to ask questions like these when he/she has learned step one and two or when you feel in your heart that your child is ready for questions like these.

When your child is learning the alphabet song, sing along with him or just play the song often, until he/she learns it. Another thing you could do to make learning the alphabet song and recognizing the twenty-six letters of the alphabet a little easier is to buy very large capital letters from your local school supply store or just visit http://www.schoolbox.com online. After you have purchased the letters, place them around your child's room or playroom as a border. Next, buy a pointer and use it to point to each letter as you and your child sing the alphabet song together. Not sure when your child is ready to learn the alphabet song? Well, when you hear your child singing along with Barney or Elmo on Sesame Street, your child is ready to learn step one. This is an incredible milestone for your child! I can remember, as if it was yesterday, teaching Chelsea how to sing the alphabet song. I couldn't believe how quickly she learned to sing the alphabet song and recognize all of the letters!

Next, I naturally started teaching her everything I could think of. She was like a sponge and loved watching programs like Sesame Street and Barney, which are great learning shows for young children. Many parents do not let their children watch television, because some of the commercials are so appalling. I agree, but there is a way around this. Many of the shows are available on DVD and are commercial free, which is ideal for families that would like to control what their kids see on television. You can buy Barney, Sesame Street, Dora the Explorer, and Gullah Gullah Island DVDs (just to name a few) for your child to watch. The great thing about buying children DVDs is that you can buy the ones you like. For example, letting your child watch a Barney video about ABCs and numbers, is a terrific way to introduce your child to the alphabet and numbers. If you are teaching your child about manners and friendships, try the Berenstain Bears DVDs. You decide which ones are good for your child. The overall goal here is to introduce your child to different things, so that he/she grows smarter each day.

As I probably have mentioned before, Chelsea was a very smart, little girl who loved learning new things. When she was encouraged and praised (which was often) she would just ham it up for me and her dad.

Nonetheless, I believe all kids are smart, and just waiting for someone to teach, encourage and praise them, too! That is why I believe all children can learn if someone has faith in them, and takes the time to teach and review with them at home.

Chelsea was learning everything as fast as I could teach it to her, so that encouraged me to start teaching her a few simple sight words like these: *a, I, me, we, see, and, cat, dog, am, the, at, to, he,* and *she.* I have also included 128 easy sight words in this book that will help your child learn to read in record time. Anyway, before I knew it, Chelsea was picking up the Dick and Jane books and reading them on her own! Just like that, she was reading at the age of three! I was so happy! I wanted to tell everyone in the world that our little girl knew how to read. From that moment on, I read to her as often as I could, and sometimes she read to me. As she grew, she became more and more comfortable with reading, and read as many beginner books she could get her little hands on. I believe this can happen for your child, too! Just work with him/her at home a little each day as I did with Chelsea, but don't forget to teach your child some other things, even after he/she learns to read. After all, learning is forever, and even as adults, we should try to learn something new everyday (or at least every week).

CHAPTER IV

Always Read To and
Work With Your Child

You should always read and work with your kids at home. It is rewarding and smart to teach your kids how to read before they start school. If we want our kids to excel in school, we have to set them up for success early. Teaching your child how to read before he/she begins school is one of the best gifts a parent can give to his/her child. Reading is a skill we all will use our entire lives.

Preparing your child for school can also be demanding of our time, but it's important that we do. To get your child ready for school, regardless of what grade he/she is going into, make sure you spend a little time each day teaching him/her something new or on next year's grade level. Some days you will read and teach. Other days, you can give your child worksheets to work on printed from www.edhelper. com. What you give your child to work on all depends on your child's age and grade level.

Is all of this beginning to sound a little overwhelming? Well, if it is starting to sound that way, remember to break things up a little. Do not try to teach your child everything all at once. You won't be able to. It is *what* you do *all along* that counts, not what you do in a couple of sessions. For an example, if your child is having a test on Friday, he/she should study as if the test is on Wednesday or Thursday. This way he/she won't have to cram for it or risk forgetting everything, as soon as the test is over. Remember, I'm big on retention. It is what your child learns and remembers that will help him/her do well on standardized tests and the SAT/ACT tests to get into college. Therefore, encourage your child to study in advance, so that he/she won't have to study so hard for tests or quizzes. Make sure your child is focusing in school, and doing all of his/her homework assignments. Remind your child to ask the teacher for help if he/she doesn't understand the homework, so he'll/she'll do better on exams and quizzes.

Now, let's talk about Joshua. I taught my son, Joshua, how to read approximately six years after I taught his sister, Chelsea, using the same techniques. I also taught many of the kids at my daycare center to read. This is why I know you are going to be successful at teaching your child how to read, too! I just know you'll get the same results. Nevertheless, I must point out that you must be committed, motivated, and determined to help your child learn to read.

As I have mentioned before, you do not have to pay someone or wait for a teacher to teach your child anything. Some expect teachers to do it all, but that's impossible! We must teach our own kids about safety, manners, values, and morals, as well as, make sure they learn to read and lots of other things. In other words, make sure your child attends church regularly, learns and obeys The Ten Commandments, and live by The Beatitudes. For those of you who may not be familiar with The Ten Commandments and The Beatitudes here they are (I believe they will help your child have self-control):

The Ten Commandments as quoted from
the *29. Precious Moments Bible*:
Exodus 20:3-17

"One-You shall have no other gods before Me.
Two-You shall not make for yourself a carved image.
Three-You shall not take the name of the LORD your God in vain.
Four-Remember the Sabbath day, to keep it holy.
Five-Honor your father and your mother.
Six-You shall not murder.
Seven-You shall not commit adultery.
Eight-You shall not steal.
Nine-You shall not bear false witness.
Ten-You shall not covet."

The BEATITUDES
Matthew 5:3-11
As quoted from the 30. *Precious*
Moment Bible

"Blessed are the poor in spirit, for theirs is the kingdom of heaven. Blessed are those who mourn, for they shall be comforted.
Blessed are the meek, for they shall inherit the earth.
Blessed are those who hunger and thirst for righteousness, for they shall be filled.
Blessed are the merciful, for they shall obtain mercy.
Blessed are the pure in heart, for they shall see God.
Blessed are the peacemakers, for they shall be called sons of God. Blessed are those who are persecuted for righteousness' sake, for theirs is the kingdom of heaven."

SAMANTHA W. DAVIS

Well, let's continue the conversation I started previously. It takes "time" to teach someone to read. Time some teachers just don't have to give to one child. So, do yourself, your child, and his/her future teachers a favor, teach your own child how to read *early*. I can't stress this fact enough. All I can tell you is that you will be glad that you took the time to teach your child how to read before sending him/her to school. Why take a chance on your child being the one who has to be sent out of the classroom to learn how to read in later grades (and that is--if someone notices that your child can't read)? So, please pay attention to your child, and give him/her schoolwork at home to complete, then you'll see for yourself what he/she knows or needs to learn. Another great tip, is to buy different workbooks on your child's grade level and upcoming grade level from a teacher supply store (just Google™ the nearest location to you), and have him/her work out of them at home, on vacation, and everywhere else he/she goes. A good idea is to keep a stack in the car, and especially on long drives.

Just as schoolchildren need time to process what they are learning at school, teaching someone how to read takes time, too. Therefore, if you spend a little time each day reading to and teaching your child the reading steps in this book, he/she will eventually learn how to read.

You know something, kids may never tell us, but they retain information better when they are taught information over time. Come to think about it, you simply retain more knowledge when you learn things all along versus learning everything all at once. With this in mind, make sure your child spend a good amount of time on any new concepts that you introduce to him/her or that he/she learns at school.

We all have heard at one time or another that teachers are underpaid for all the work they do. That is why it's important for us to remind our kids to listen and pay attention in class.

If we could get our kids to do this consistently, they will learn more and score better on tests. In addition, parents should teach their kids extra skills throughout the school year and prepare them for the next grade during the summer. I know I have said this before, but I'm going to keep repeating it. It is important that we do these things for our kids if we want them to succeed in school and in the future. If we can persuade our kids to behave in school, the teachers can teach our kids more, and the more our kids know the further they'll go. Remember knowledge is powerful, and "a mind is a terrible thing to waste" according to the United Negro College Fund http://www.uncf.org, and I concur. Therefore, we have no other choice, but to insist that our kids go to school everyday and learn what the teachers are trying to teach them. This way our kids will have the skills they'll need to go after their dreams. Therefore, we do not have an option here. We *must* encourage our kids to do their best and work with them at home almost everyday, starting on the first day of kindergarten all the way to graduation day. This way, they'll be prepared to get into college, go into the service, or start technical school. You can start today teaching and working with your kids at home, by printing off worksheets from www.edhelper.com that will teach or introduce them to new skills and facts. We have to do these things for our kids, if we want them to succeed in the future. It's really up to us, to make sure our kids are learning from their teachers, and that we are supplementing their education, by teaching our kids more things at home. Teaching your child how to read early, will also help him/her learn different things easier. Besides, reading is the foundation of learning.

I believe helping kids develop strong reading and math skills will help them do better in school and on tests. All you have to do is make learning a priority in your home, and your child will be successful in everything he/she does.

The most important thing to keep in mind is that our children are depending on us to help them develop and grow. Whether we realize it or not, we play an integral part in our kids' futures, and much of what we say and do each day can determine what direction their lives take. With this in mind, teach your kids something new everyday.

Reading is a wonderful thing to be able to do. Reading can teach you so many things in a roundabout way. You can travel to new places, and learn about other cultures without boarding one plane or train. Books can also inspire, motivate, and entertain you. So, read something every day to your child, and if he/she can read by himself/herself, encourage him/her to read a little every single day, too.

Teaching your child how to read can be very easy for some but difficult for others. If you find yourself having a hard time teaching your child how to read, take a deep breath and exhale. Don't worry-- it will get easier. Sometimes, all it takes is for us to believe in our kids for them to succeed. Nevertheless, every child can learn to read, if someone is willing to put in the time to teach and work with him/her.

You know something; your child is going to be starting kindergarten before you know it. That is exactly how fast time goes sometimes. You know the saying, "Time flies when you're having fun.", and we always have fun watching babies grow. That is why we must read to our babies and toddlers and teach them new things all the time, to give them a head start in kindergarten one day.

Try putting together a home schedule to follow at home that includes practicing music, working on math, reading, learning vocabulary, and working on websites like ixl.com and clicknkids.com (use samanthadavis@comcast.net to receive a discount on this website), to keep your child ahead in school. A good time to start a schedule like this is around three and a half years old or sooner. It will also help you remember to teach your child something new everyday at home and it will also get your child used to following a school schedule.

Giving your child an early education at home, along with some extra curricular activities like sports and music, can help build your child's self-confidence.

Did you know according to Dr. D. James Kennedy, "Sending children to public schools and {expecting} schools to teach them everything is a relatively recent development? From the 1600's until the mid 19th century parents maintained responsibility for their children's education." *(5. The Daily Encouraging Word)* As I have referenced before, we cannot depend on schools to teach our kids everything they need to know, nor can we rely on them to teach our children good old-fashioned manners.

Here are some things your child can do to make sure he succeeds in school: listen to his/her teacher, keep his/her hands to himself/herself, limit bathroom breaks, participate in class, sit up front, do his/her homework on time, and be punctual and attend school each day.

Make learning at home fun and exciting, because if you do, your child will want to learn something new everyday and addition to doing his/her homework. Another great thing to do is to cheer your child on as he/she learns new things. Children are like sponges. They soak up knowledge as quick as you can teach it to them. Children, as I've stated before are a lot smarter than we think they are. Their minds are like little computers, just waiting to be filled. We have to make sure our kids' minds are filled with good things, too.

Kids pay more attention than we think they do, and they are always in the state of learning. That is why it's important to create an environment conducive to learning, because whether we know it or not our kids are taking it all in. For instance, one day while sitting in the family room looking at the world globe, my youngest child points to Jamaica and exclaims, "That's where Usain Bolt lives!" It took me a moment to realize he was talking about the sprinter from Jamaica, who won three gold medals for being the fastest man in the world during the 2008 Summer Olympics. This example proves that children are always learning, either directly or indirectly. Therefore, it is wise to be aware of what our children are exposed to at home and away from home.

Playing trivia games with your kids is also a fantastic way to teach them new things. It's a great activity for the entire family to do together! It's also a wonderful way to keep the lines of communication open with your children. Two great games to give a try are Tip of the Tongue tm and Don't Quote Me tm. I like carrying trivia questions around with me and especially on long trips. Sometimes, if my husband is driving, I take out my trivia cards and announce, "Let's play Family Trivia!" After everyone groans (just kidding), I announce the category and ask questions from the deck of cards. Everyone in the car tries guessing the answer, including dad. The game is over when everyone gets tired of playing the game. As a result, you'll get brighter kids, a smarter family, and some new memories. A game like Trivia is just the perfect game to foster family involvement, too. The ice is broken when the younger kids can't believe mom, dad, or an older sibling doesn't *remember* an answer to a particular question. One more thing, if you have very young children, try asking questions on their age level.

You really can teach your child how to read and give him/her a great head start in school without paying someone else to do it. All you have to do is work with your child at home for at least 30 minutes a day. Teach him/her things like how to read, how to spell and write, and how to add and subtract early to give him/her a great head start in elementary school. Next, just continue teaching your child new things, as well as review what he/she has already learned to keep him/her ahead in school and in the grades ahead.

I can't stress enough how important it is for us to encourage our kids to do their best in school and help them regardless of what grade they are in. We can do more than just encourage them to do well; we can also enroll them in learning centers like Kumon™ or Sylvan™ to supplement their education, if it is in your budget to do so. Educational CDs and DVDs can also be used to teach your child new things at home and make him/her smarter. That is why it's imperative that we get involved in our kids' education to make sure that we are doing everything in our power to help our kids excel in school and get brighter. After all, every parent wants the best for their children, and it all begins at home. Therefore, we must begin today making sure that our kids receive a quality education by reading, teaching and reviewing with our kids at home.

It's my opinion, that teachers don't have the time to teach students the way they would like to. One way we can help them is to review with our kids at home. For an example, if your child just learned multiplication facts last year in math, take some time to review them with him/her at home. A smart way to review multiplication, adding, subtraction, and division facts is to give your child some worksheets to work on or to have him/her work on www.ixl.com. Don't forget to go over the worksheets with your child to help him/her correct any mistakes he/she may have made. When we review with our kids at home, teachers can move on and teach other lessons that need to be taught. Many times, teachers can't move forward because they are reviewing facts and skills that the students should already know.

Just so, you'll know, I have used Kumon™ in the past and was very pleased with their services; however, I stopped using Kumon™ because I wanted to try out a few of my own techniques. Well, they worked, and now I use my own techniques, tips, and strategies, along with some of the websites I've referenced in this book. Nevertheless, you can use my techniques, in addition to using Kumon™ or Sylvan's™ services. I think it is a good idea to supplement all learning, for a well-rounded education. In my opinion, a quality education is a combination of different educational experiences and exposures.

I think kids learn better, when we make learning and reading fun and rewarding. I think it's inspiring when we reward our kids for doing well in school. Challenging your child to read 50 books to earn a summer vacation to Disney World is a wonderful way to encourage your child to read more. You are going to take him/her anyway, so why not make him/her earn it? You'll have a smarter child walking around Disney World if you do, and you'll be a happier parent (smile).

Don't allow your kids to make you feel guilty about giving them extra schoolwork over the summer, either. It's a strategy kids like to use, when they want to get out of doing extra schoolwork. Just remember that kids will naturally pout and complain when it come to learning sometimes, because *children* will protest from time to time. Remind your kids that there are kids around the world that attend school year round. Don't feel guilty about making your kids read and learn new skills over the summer or anytime during the year. Just stay focused on the goal (and that is giving your child a real head start in everything) and remind your kids that you are making sure they learn and do well in school now, so that they will get careers of their own and take care of themselves one day. They may not thank you now mom and dad, but they will thank you when they are older.

Keep in mind, we won't be the only parents encouraging our kids to read, learn, and review over the summer. This isn't anything new. There have always been parents who work with their kids at home, to keep them college bound. So, make sure your child continues to work on new skills throughout the year and during his/her summer break, so that he/she will be college bound, too. Send your child back to school in the fall mom and dad with new clothes and new skills, because it's our job to mold and groom our kids for their future.

Every summer you work with your child, you're increasing his/her chances of graduating from high school and going off to college one day. Summer gives your child a break from the daily routine of things, but it's also a great time to help him/her get ready for the upcoming school year. Working with your child over the summer may mean something different from one family to the next. For your family, it may mean taking your child to basketball practice, Kumon, and to piano lessons. For another family, it may mean actually sitting down at the kitchen table and going over math problems or introducing your child to a new language using Rosetta Stone software or a combination of the two. Truthfully, it doesn't matter what your child works on or improves over the summer, as long as he uses some of his/her summer, reading, learning, and reviewing.

Did you know that there are resources in your community that you can use to help your child develop and grow? These resources will help your child learn new things and become more knowledgeable about the world. A good place to find out what's being offered right in your own neighborhood is to start with your local newspaper and library. You'll be surprised to find out how many resources are available in your area. Some of them may have a small fee, but many of them do not. Take advantage of the resources that are free first, but don't let the small fees scare you away, either. Sometimes, you can find a way around certain fees, and a little creativity can go a long way. Many times, you'll find scholarships available for students who test well or discounts based on a family's total income. For instance, you may find that you can give your child a couple of dance lessons free, just for asking for a trial class. Although, it may merely be a couple of classes, at least you would have given your child an experience she/he won't soon forget. Ask if the dance studio would consider offering your child a full or partial dance scholarship, because many times, they can right it off around tax time. It doesn't hurt to ask, and you'll never know what you can get if you don't ask. More importantly, take advantage of all the programs being offered at your library, park, community resource center, nearby businesses, and churches. For instance, your local library may offer free chess classes, test preparation for the PSAT and SAT, and free foreign language lessons on line. For that reason, don't overlook these resources, they could be a gold mine.

Your community park may offer some of their sport programs free or at discounted prices. Again, you will never know, unless you ask. Don't forget to read your town's newspaper for free admission to concerts, theatres, art festivals, and museums throughout the year. The internet is also a smart resource of educational websites that can help your child learn new things. Websites like, nationalzoo. si.edu, Smithsonian.org/museums/, www.nature.nps.gov/ views/inex.cfm, www.upm.com, www.planetinaction.com, and earth.google.com/intl/en/ are great sites to have your child explore. In addition, if you live in Atlanta, Georgia check out Atlanta Parent magazine. It's a great parenting magazine that lists many events and attractions happening throughout the school year and during the summer. You can also view their magazine online at www.atlantaparent.com.

I believe every city has a parent magazine, so don't forget to ask your local library about the magazine's availability.

Therefore, all parents have the power within them to help their child succeed in school and in other activities. If you have a will to help your child achieve his/her dreams, then you'll find a way to make it happen. Never forget the number one resource that every child has at his/her fingertips. It's free, effective, and always available. That resource is YOU!

Yes, it will take a lot of work, and as I mentioned before, your kids may even protest, but don't give in. So, don't forget to have your kids read and learn new things over the summer, because the pace is a lot slower and a wonderful time to get ahead. Keep learning fun and remember to incorporate a few mini vacations, and your kids will enjoy learning over their summer break.

I have put many examples throughout this book that will help keep your child on track to getting a real head start in school. All you have to do is put them into practice to help your child learn to read early, along with learning how to add and subtract, write, draw and color, and lots of other things, before starting school. Don't grow weary about making sure your child does well in school, because there are some who believe kids should just play all day. Well, I'm one of them; however, I also believe children should be nurtured with lots of love and hugs, a good education, morals, manners, and with the conviction that they can grow up to be anything they want to be. Besides, the smarter our kids get, the more opportunities they'll have in the future.

You know something, sometimes others won't always get why you are insisting that your child does: his/her homework, eats healthy, does extra reading, and study to do well on tests and quizzes. Don't let that discourage you. Some will argue that grades aren't everything, but that just isn't true. Well, does it matter or not that your doctor passes his/her medical licensing examination? Of course, it matters. This is my point exactly. Grades do matter and our kids should be encouraged to make the best grades they can. As I've referenced before, good grades are an indication that your child is learning something, attending school regularly, turning in assignments on time, doing his/her homework, and cares a whole lot. Therefore, your child *should* be held accountable for how he/she performs in school. I know you are probably thinking my mom or dad never had to make sure I did well in school. Well, that's probably true; however, times are different. We have to make sure our kids are brought up to meet the challenges of today and tomorrow's world.

Before I go on, I wanted to reference my Father-in-law, the late Mr. Lewis Davis, CPA for becoming the first African-American Certified Public Accountant in Miami, Florida. Every year The FICPA Educational Foundation holds an annual 1040K run/walk during the spring to reward accounting students scholarship money to continue pursuing their accounting goals. For more information go to http://www.ficpa.org/Content/EdFoundation/Events/1040K.aspx or http://www.active.com/running/miami-fl/ficpa-k-2011. Who knows maybe your child will become the next CPA in his/her town?

In the future, our children will need a college degree with job training just to land an adequate job. According to an article posted on The Huffington Post, *48. http://www.huffingtonpost.com/2010/05/09/obama-at-hampton-universi_n_569258.html*, President Obama said, "…in the past, a high school diploma was a ticket to a solid middle-class life, but not anymore." How true this statement is today. Most *great* jobs today require a bachelor's degree or higher. Therefore, you can just imagine how it will be in the future. As a result, parents who are insisting that their kids do well in class, and treat others the way they would like to be treated, are doing their kids a service. So, keep encouraging your child to do well in school, by making sure he/she is listening in class, taking excellent notes, and is preparing for all tests and quizzes wholeheartedly. If we do not help our children succeed and encourage them to do their best, our kids can be potentially left behind.

Remember, we're at war. We're fighting for a quality education for our children, and we will win by working with our kids at home, one child at a time. Some school districts are unfortunately cutting school programs like: music, art, computers, and foreign language classes. This is why it is up to us to arm our kids with skills and knowledge that will help them compete in tomorrow's world. Let's stay committed in helping our kids achieve. We can and we will! Starting today, make it your mission to make sure that your child is learning at school, and is making, as many A's as possible. Why should we encourage our kids to make A's? Well, in my opinion, an A says that your child learned at least 90% of what was taught in class, but if he/she earns a B, that's okay, too. Just keep encouraging your child to do his/her best in class always.

We have to help our kids achieve in and out of the classroom, too! That is why I believed President Obama's mother allegedly woke him up every morning at 4:00 in the morning to go over English lessons for three whole hours! It was important to her that he did well in school.

It is not enough to send your child to an assumed "good school", and then leave his/her education entirely in someone else's hand. What's important is that your child learns most of what is being taught in each class, regardless of what school he/she attends. Many kids have attended public schools and have become successful businesspersons, doctors, principals, lawyers, entrepreneurs, teachers, politicians, and authors. It isn't about the school; it's about the student who applies himself/herself. You can increase your child's odds of succeeding in class by encouraging him/her to review his/her class notes often and read the assigned chapters (and some cases encourage your child to read more, if he/she has time). Encourage your child to do his/her homework everyday, as well; it can improve your child's chances of making an A or B in class.

Some people don't care what grade their child makes in class, just as long as he/she is going to school everyday and passing to the next grade. I disagree with this kind of thinking, because children should be taught that it does matter how you do in class. For instance, let's say Dr. Ace passed all of his classes in medical school with an 88 or higher, and Dr. OK passed all of his classes with a 70 and the highest grade he ever received was an 83 in just one of his classes. Which doctor would you like operating on you, if you found yourself in need of an operation? I think most of us would choose Dr. Ace, who obviously passed all of his classes with an A or B. So, in my opinion, I have proven my point again, that grades do matter. Here's an example of why we should encourage our kids to do their best. Let's say your child gets an 80 in math for the year, and you're happy because he/she passed, right? Well, if you'll take a closer look with me, you'll find that your child didn't learn 20% of the material taught in class. That means in next year's math class he/she will start the year off knowing only 80% of the 100% he/she was expected to learn. It doesn't seem like a big deal right now, but that 20% percent can translate into your child struggling in math for an entire school year. The good news is that you can make sure your child learns the 20% over the summer, by collaborating with his/her teacher. It's a good thing we have the summers to see to it that our kids brush up on their skills, isn't it? Here's another example: Parent Z is a "new school" parent who doesn't stress out over grades, in fact, the only thing that matters to this parent is that his/her child is enjoying school and is passing every year. If his/her child receives a 73 in English, for instance, Parent Z is okay with that, because all he/she is concern about is that his/her child enjoys school each day and passes to the next grade. What he/she doesn't realize is that his/her child didn't learn 27% of the material taught in English class all year! So, as you can see, it does matter what grade your child makes in class, because good grades mean your child is obviously learning most of what is being taught in class (which will help him/her stay college bound). On the other hand, we have to be flexible and understanding, after all, (as mentioned before) our kids are children, not saints; that being said, our kids are not going to always do as well as we would like them to do on their report cards, tests, finals, and standardized tests. Nevertheless, it isn't the end of the world; we still have time to work with our kids at home, and it shows them that we care. For an example, if you encourage your child to make an "A", but he/she brings home an 87 instead, *this is good mom and dad*, because if he/she wasn't working hard enough to get an A, he/she could have ended up with a lower grade. Therefore, always encourage your child to do his/her best in everything he/she does; however, if your child ends up with more B's than A's on his/her report card, applaud his/her efforts, and continue to encourage him/her to do his/her best. Now, on a rare occasion (hopefully), your child may end up with a C or maybe even two C's on his/her report card (ouch!) don't panic, I've experienced this! What you want to do going forward, is work with your child and your child's teacher or hire a tutor for him/her. Enrolling him/her in Kumon™ or Sylvan™ isn't a bad idea at this point, either. Nevertheless, we should never give up on encouraging our kids to do their best in everything they do. We should never let our kids get used to seeing C's on their report card, because we know that our kids can do better than a C. Remember, C is merely passing the class. It says your child did an okay job in the class. Yes, it's a passing grade, but we cannot encourage mediocrity or complacency. We wouldn't tolerate this from our favorite restaurant, or ourselves, so why should we allow it from our kids? So, let's encourage our kids to reach for the stars, and if by chance they don't reach them, at least they'll land on the moon.

In order for your child to do well in school, it is going to take a lot of effort from your child. Nevertheless, you can help and encourage him/her by asking questions like, "Do you have a quiz this week?" or "Do you have a test coming up?" Parent involvement like this is the kind kids respect, because kids respect what you inspect (as stated before).

Ask your kids this simple question to remind them to do their best in school, "What do you want to be when you grow up?" If they don't know yet, that's okay. Your goal is to get them thinking about what they want to be when they grow up, so it will motivate them to do their best in school. Keep in mind our kids have it in them, to become anything they want to be. We all know that in order to succeed, we all have to decide to become great at something. Therefore, we must always encourage our kids to do their very best.

If our kids are aspiring to attend college one day, we must encourage them to be good students now. In order to succeed in college, one must have great study habits and a willingness to learn. That is why it is so important to encourage our kids to excel in school now, so that they will excel in college in the future.

It's also a good idea to have your kids write down their goals and to hang them up in plain view for everyone to see. This will remind them to do their best in everything, so that their dreams will come true. For an example, our son has told us that he wants to become a professional athlete and a judge. First, we congratulated him on making up his mind what he wants to do in the future. Secondly, we told him to write down his goals, and put them up in his room. Lastly, we told him to look at them often to remind him to work hard in school and on the field and court. Then, every chance we get, we enroll him in different sport programs, to help him hone his skills. We also remind him to do well in school, so that he can go to law school one day.

In my opinion, kids who are aspiring to become singers, entertainers or professional athletes should always be encouraged to do well in school, too. This way they'll be more prepared to handle the business part of these careers and have a backup plan if things don't work out as planned. Nevertheless, always remember to encourage your kids in their pursuits and remind them that *anything is possible*. Most of all let them know that you believe in them.

On the other hand, our daughter has expressed to us that she would like to become a children's doctor or a lawyer, and we congratulated her, as we did Joshua. We also suggested she write down these goals and go after them with all her might. We did ask her to think of something else she would like to become, just in case her first two choices don't work out. We suggested this, because she is in the tenth grade, and is closer to going off to college than Joshua is. You see, we don't believe in sugar coating anything for our kids. We would rather be up front and forthcoming with them, so that they will have a better chance at achieving their goals. We believe our kids can become anything they want to become, but we also believe in having some great back up plans. I've had to use them, and I'm sure many of you have had to, too. For an example, I was talking to a mom and dad the other day that was very proud of their son, who had just graduated from college. I learned later that their son had initially gone to college to become a doctor, but ended up with a Bachelor's degree in Dietetics and Nutrition instead. Well, how awesome is that! My point is that their son had a backup plan, because sometimes things don't work out as you plan them. However, it was a degree, he could be proud of achieving. Nonetheless, we must be honest and forthcoming with our children, so that they'll set realistic goals for themselves and work towards achieving them.

Remember, it's never too early for your child to get a head start on their careers. Just think about it for a moment. Many actors, professional athletes, and musicians have been working at their professions since they were kids. They have invested many years perfecting their skills of acting, singing, and sport of choice. Consequently, just like these professionals who obviously worked on their skills early, we can also encourage our kids to do the same. For an example, if your child wants to become a professional athlete, enroll him/her in sports, take him/her to games, practice with him/her at home, and show him/her that you believe in him/her by putting his/her best on www.youtube.com like Justin Bieber's mom did. If your child wants to become a singer or musician, give him/her singing and music lessons, take him/her to see other musicians and singers perform, and encourage him/her to practice at home. You might also think about putting his/her best performances on www.youtube.com, as well, or encourage him/her to create an app of his best acts and put them on itunes.com for sale.

Another example, if your child wants to become a business professional, dentist, doctor, nurse, business owner, real estate agent, lawyer, teacher, or an author, it's a good idea to take him/her to see some of these professionals at work. Another idea is to have your child do research on what he/she wants to become when he/she grows up. This will get him/her thinking about what he/she can do now to help him/her reach his/her goals. You can also buy games that will introduce your child to his/her future career or enroll him/her in programs that will give him/her a head start on becoming a _____(fill in the blank with what your child wants to be when he/she grows up).

Whatever you do, remind your kids, as they pursue their goals, that every goal begins with a winning attitude and good grades are always helpful. Why am I stressing good grades again, because colleges and potential employers will want to know how your child performed in school? Like I mentioned before, grades, just like credit follows you everywhere you go, and can tell others a lot about you, without you even being present. Good grades can open doors for you, just like good credit can. Good marks can say a lot about a potential employee or college student. Therefore, remind your kids, to make good grades in school, because you never have to explain success, but you always have to explain failure.

Everyone knows that no one gives out good grades, they are earned, and a lot of work goes into accomplishing them. Therefore, as I've just mentioned, no one has to explain success, just failure, and as the old saying goes, "If you fail to plan, you plan to fail." Take into account, your goal, as a parent is to do everything in your power to help your child achieve his/her goals by encouraging him/her every step of the way. Think about it, you only get one chance to raise your kids, so raise them well. As I've mentioned before, your kids will try to push back, when you are encouraging them to read a book or learn something new. Nevertheless, we have to do what is best for our children, and sometimes telling them no, isn't always easy. However, we have to make them accountable for their "own" goals. If your kids sulk about doing extra schoolwork at home, just remind them that encouraging them to do it isn't a walk in the park for you, either.

Your kids may grow up and become the next Michael Jordan, President Bill Clinton, Colin Powell, President Barack Obama and First Lady Michelle Obama, Dr. Martin Luther King, Jr., Coretta Scott-King, Oprah Winfrey, Hillary Clinton, Bill Gates, Celine Dion, Steve Jobs, Babe Ruth or the next "big name" others will reference in a book someday. Therefore, work with your kids at home, in sports, music, and in other activities, and who knows your child might just grow up and become somebody worth admiring, too!

I know I have said this before, but we can't just hope everything works out okay for our kids. We have to raise our kids with good manners and with a quality education, because this is what it is going to take for our kids to succeed in the future.

I believe that every child can receive a quality education at any school, because getting a quality education depends on the child's willingness to learn. Abraham Lincoln gave himself a quality education, with limited resources, that is why I believe that all Americans can get a quality education, if they are self-motivated and self-disciplined enough. A quality education begins in the home. We have to teach our kids different things at home. We simply can't wait for teachers to teach our kids everything anymore. The World Wide Web has open up an endless supply of resources that can help us teach our kids at home. Yet, you should send your kids to school each day, in addition to teaching them extra things at home. In my opinion, the formula to obtaining a quality education is parent involvement, additional learning at home, enrollment at a learning center, and making good grades and having good manners in school. So, keep encouraging your child to do his/her best in everything, so that he/she will have a real chance of accomplishing his/her goals one day.

CHAPTER V

Consistency is the Key

This book is designed for parents with schoolchildren in grades K-12th. It really doesn't matter how old your kids are, because it is never too late or too early to give them a real head start in school and in life. You can also teach your kids how to read, if he/she doesn't know how to, yet, by putting the reading steps in this book into practice. In addition, this book will inspire and persuade you to encourage your kids to do their best at school each day, and will show you how to give your kids the best head start ever and why you must.

Keep in mind, consistency is the key. After all, it is the mother of invention and progress. If Benjamin Franklin wasn't consistent, he might not have discovered electricity. One way you can be consistent in helping your child get smarter, is to encourage him/her to read something new everyday. If your child isn't old enough to read on his/her own or hasn't learned to read yet, read to him/her regularly. As you read to your child, bring unfamiliar words to his/her attention, this will help him/her learn new words. Do not forget to have your older children read to you as well, to see how they are progressing along with their reading skills. You should also encourage your older kids to read as if they were acting in a play. It will help your child speak with lots of inflection and meaning, which is a great way to train them to speak.

If your child hasn't learned how to read yet, just continue teaching him/her how to read using the easy reading steps in this book. Make sure he/she can recognize and say each letter, as well as, review the sounds of the alphabet with him/her. After he/she learns the letters and sounds of the alphabet, teach him what vowels and consonants are. Next, teach him some easy sight words like a, I, he, she, we, you, to, too, be, cat, dog, mom, dad, bee, be, no, yes, can, go, and do. When your child learns every letter, the sound each letter makes, the difference between a vowel and a consonant, and can say a few sight words, don't be surprised if all of a sudden he/she starts reading all by himself/herself.

Another way to be consistent in helping your child become and stay ahead is by motivating your child to be excellent at everything, and never giving up on your child. You can also give him extra schoolwork at home. If we teach our kids new things at home, and encourage them to do well in school, our kids more than likely will succeed. Besides, if every child could start kindergarten knowing how to write, read, draw, and do arithmetic, our kids would be in a position to do extremely well in school. So, teach and review basic learning skills with your child at home before he starts school. Now, all you have to do is continue reviewing and teaching your child new things during the school year and over the summer break, to keep him/her ahead.

In addition to getting ahead for school, it is just as important to make sure our kids know our names, their home phone number, and their home address before starting kindergarten. You'll be surprised to know how many kids start second grade without knowing their home phone number or address. It's a good idea to have them practice writing their contact information at home. If kids can learn how to play a computer game or send a text on a cell phone at five years old or older, then they certainly can learn their contact information. What if they get lost one day, would they know how to tell someone where they live? Who their parents are? What is their phone number? Parents we need to teach our kids things like this and more in today's world! Talk to your children, to find out what they know or do not know. It may surprise you. If you like what you hear, great, if you don't, then teach your kids what they should know, like their contact information, in case, they ever get lost.

I hope I am encouraging you to take charge of your child's education and to be unswerving about giving him/her a head start in school and in everything else. Some of the things we can do to get involved in our child's education, in addition to giving him/her extra schoolwork at home and enrolling him/her in a learning center like Kumon™, is to become a part of the PTA (Parents Teachers Association) and attend most of the meetings if you can. We can also volunteer in our child's classroom or donate learning materials or other things that are needed. We can also ask the teacher if she needs assistance with anything. We can do all of these things and more to get involved in our child's education.

We have to encourage our kids to make getting good grades in school a priority. We have to insist that our kids do their best in school, because there is no way around it. Doing something as simple as sitting down with your child regularly to see what they are learning in school can help your child reach his/her destination, one day at a time.

I think all kids have it in them to become something great. They just have to be nurtured and encouraged. One thing to keep in mind is that our kids are individuals, and they will become what they want to become when they grow up. We can't force our dreams onto our children. For an example, if you wanted to be a famous singer, you can't force your child to become one. Your child has his/her own life to live. What we *can do* is believe in our kids and let them know that they can become anything they want to become, if they are willing to work hard or smart enough to become it.

The advice in this book will help you be consistent in helping your child achieve his goals. Keep in mind, some kids love distractions (including chores), anything that will keep them from sitting down and learning something or doing their homework. They will even try to distract you mom and dad, hoping you won't notice that *they are not* doing their homework. Don't fall for any of this! Stay alert! Kids are not only smart, but they can be sly as a fox, too. Some of them are masters at distracting teachers, also! So, make sure your kids stay in the race, so to speak.

You can also be confident that you're receiving some great advice in this book, because I've used all the tips and strategies I'm suggesting you use. I've actually used every step and suggestion in this book, and my kids are proof that they work. I have also learned from trial and error, what works and what doesn't. Now, all you have to do is benefit from what works.

So, what do you think? Is it better to learn from someone who has learned from trial and error, or from someone who has just learned it in a textbook or from some university? I think you would agree with me that most people would rather take advice from someone who has actually used the tips they are suggesting.

For an example, back in the 1800's during President Thomas Jefferson's time, people thought tomatoes were poison (Can you believe this?). Well, according to history, no one ate tomatoes until Thomas Jefferson tried them and didn't die. Get it? He didn't just tell them that the tomatoes weren't poison; he "tried" them and proved to everyone that they were not poison. *(6. "Don't Know Much about the Presidents" by Kenneth C. Davis)* Can you imagine eating salads today without tomatoes or a BLT sandwich without tomatoes? If you do not like tomatoes, you probably could care less; however, for the rest of us, I am bringing up this bit of history to make my point that people are willing to try something at least once, if it worked out okay for someone else.

The methods in this book not only worked with my own children. They also worked with the children at my learning center, as well. This may sound like it's too good to be true, but it is. More importantly, you can use these methods with your own children, too! If you take just a few minutes a day implementing the steps in this book and putting the suggestions into practice, your child is going to learn how to read plus a whole lot more!

Don't forget to read to your child as you teach him/ her how to read, it will help familiarize him/her with the written word. So, stay consistent and motivated and your child will learn how to read one-step at a time. When you read to your child, while you are teaching him/her how to read, it can also help him/her learn other things. Now then, read something to your child every single day.

As mentioned earlier, it is important to talk, sing, read, and play classical music for your baby. It's also critical because babies are impressionable, especially during the first thirty-six months of their lives. Picture books with few words are perfect books to read to your very young children. If you keep this up regularly, you're going to have a little Einstein on your hands very soon. So, just stay consistent and do something everyday that will teach your toddler how to read, and give him/her a great head start in kindergarten someday.

CHAPTER VI

You Are Your Child's First Teacher

I once thought about opening an after-school program to teach kids how to read, along with some other basic skills. My staff and I would have taught the kids good study habits, organizational skills, and speaking skills to make them better students. It also would have been mandatory for every high school student to take self-esteem and college preparatory classes. Homework study hall would have been an ongoing requirement for every child at the center, as an effort to boost every child's grades at school. Furthermore, the kids who did a brilliant job on their report cards would have been given awards every marking period, to encourage all the kids at the center to do their best in school. An after-school program like this, in my opinion, is just the kind of center we need in our communities to help America's kids do well in school.

Well, after a lot of thought, I decided to write a book instead. This way, I could encourage thousands of parents to do the things I would have done if I had opened an after-school center, in their own homes. The ideas, tips, and suggestions in this book will help parents give their kids a jump-start in school. This book will also inspire parents to teach their children how to read, write, and do arithmetic before they start school. This book will also motivate parents to continue working with their kids in grades K-12th. Remember, you are your child's first teacher, and you can teach your child anything you put your mind to.

I truly believe all children can learn and do well in school. All we would have to do is take advantage of the first five years of your child's life and teach them how to read, do arithmetic, count, write, identify shapes, colors, and more!

You should have no reservations about helping your child become smarter. Just continue putting the tips of this book into practice and your child will become a very well read student. All you have to do is set some time aside each day and read to or with your child as often as you can. I strongly believe that children, who are read to a lot, will not only learn how to read but will also learn many different things.

If your child is very young and does not understand what you are reading to him/her, that's okay. What's important is that you're reading to your child, and he/she is listening and learning. We must always remember that kids are always in the state of learning, so read, read, read to them. I cannot emphasize this enough, but it's important for you to read to or with your child as often as you can, at least twice a day.

Many children right now are living in households that believe schools are responsible for teaching their kids everything. Although schools are accountable for teaching our kids a great deal, they simply cannot teach our kids everything *they will learn*. It really does take mom, dad, pastor, teacher, coach, grandma, grandpa, and the village to teach and raise our kids. Therefore, start teaching your kids today many things, and don't forget to give him/her a head start in other activities like sports, music, dance, cheerleading, drama, art, gymnastics, and especially reading.

We must encourage our kids to learn at school, and we must insist they do some extra schoolwork at home. Parents have to take an active role in teaching their own children how to read, count, draw, and write before they start school, and continue working with them throughout the school year. As well as, teach them about the world they live in, other cultures, animals, plants, and so much more. A parent who is actively involved in their child's education is really giving their child a head start in school. Each year, many kids get the opportunity to attend learning centers like Kumon™ and Sylvan™ to enhance their education. Although these centers can give your child an advantage in math and reading, the fees can be insurmountable for some families. Therefore, if you are in a position to enroll your child in a center like these, by all means, do it. Centers like these can really help your child do well in school, but the websites cited in this book are just as effective, if you have your child work on them a little each day. Nevertheless, these centers should never take the place of parent or family involvement, and if your child is enrolled in one of these centers, you should continue working with him/her at home (--like giving him/her some extra reading to do).

I believe reading books on a number of different topics can make your child knowledgeable about many different things. As you can see, time is of the essence, and it's important to teach our kids new things like: language, vocabulary, arithmetic, science, music, and art before they are required to go to school. Teaching your child concepts like these early, along with reading can give him a solid foundation to stand on at school.

Think about it for a moment, if a child doesn't learn how to read before starting school, he/she could potentially be left behind. Come with me and let's define the word "read" for a moment. Did you know that the word "read" according to the *43. Microsoft Word Processor dictionary* means to interpret written material? It also means according to the *44. Microsoft Word Processor dictionary*-- to be "informed or provided with knowledge through reading". As you can see, one can become very smart from just reading. Did you know the word "read" also means-- to say the words of written or printed material aloud? Therefore, teaching your child how to read before he/she starts school is just a smart thing to do. Do you really want your kids going to school one day, having to catch up with the other kids? Playing catch up can be extremely frustrating for any child and their parents. You cannot allow this to happen to your kids. You have no other choice but to teach your kids how to read, write, and to do arithmetic before they begin kindergarten.

Let's ponder another thought. If your child didn't know how to read before starting kindergarten, he/she wouldn't be able to read the instructions on a worksheet in class or the teacher's name on the board. Then, your child may become discouraged if most of the kids in class were reading, and he/she wasn't. This is why it is crucial that you teach your child how to read the written word before sending him/her off to school.

Many kids are beginning school with reading, writing, and math skills these days, and that is why I'm motivating you to give your child this kind of head start, too. If your child doesn't begin school with these skills, it may put a damper on his/her educational experience. Right now, there are parents who are working with their children to make them smarter, and these are the very kids your children will be competing with in college and on the job. In my opinion, these kids are setting the bar, and can potentially be leaving most of the kids behind in school. Therefore, educate your kids at home, and teach them skills that will give them an advantage in school. I believe children who start school reading, starts school with an advantage. Therefore, we must give our kids a great head start in school, if we want their dreams to come true. Therefore, continue working with your kids at home to give them a jump-start in school and keep them ahead by continuing to teach them new things throughout the school year. If you cannot do it, then pay someone else to do it, because this is better than doing nothing at all.

Another reason I was so inspired to write this book was to encourage parents everywhere to support their children's efforts in school, but in extra-curricular activities, too. Not only should you teach your child how to read, and many other things, you should also give him/her a head start in sports, music, dance, theatre, gymnastics, and in almost anything, you can think of right now. Developing skills in music and in sports can boost a child's self-esteem and confidence. So, enroll your child in sports and in music today.

Enrolling your child in a sport will also help him/her get his/her move on, visit www.letsmove.gov to find out more. *Letsmove.gov* was created by our First Lady Michelle Obama to encourage kids, parents, and everyone to eat healthier and exercise everyday. This is an excellent idea, and parents everywhere should model the way for their kids, by eating more salads, lean meats, whole grains, fruits, lean dairy and by exercising every single day.

By now, you should have a deeper understanding of why I believe schools cannot be held entirely responsible for what our kids learn. We cannot wait for teachers to teach our children how to read, do arithmetic, and write. We have to do our part, and send them to school knowing how to do these things, already. This way the teachers can build on what their students know. None of us would dream of sending our kids to elementary school without being potty trained or not knowing how to talk, would we? Of course, we wouldn't! So, let's make a change, and send our kids to kindergarten not *only* knowing how to talk, but armed with the ability to read, count, add, subtract, write, color, and draw. Can you imagine? This would be a dream to a kindergarten teacher! If kids started school knowing how to read and write, it would give our teachers a chance to teach other interesting and new things.

The fact that you bought this book says a lot about you. It says you value education and America's future (our kids). It also says you are committed to doing whatever it takes to give your child a real head start. Very good, because it is just the kind of attitude it is going to take to make sure your child succeeds in everything.

The earlier your child learns to read, the better off he/she will be, and this book contains five easy steps that will help you teach your child how to read early. You will also learn tips that will have you excited about teaching your child different things, that are guaranteed to give him/her a head start in school. After all, your child spends most of his/her time with you, so it makes a lot of sense to take some of that time and teach him/her something.

So, what are you waiting for? Begin today giving your child a real head start in school, and teach him/her how to read, write, and do arithmetic. After all, you are his/her first teacher.

CHAPTER VII

Play Dates Can Be Educational, Too

Play dates, play dates, play dates! Have you ever planned a play date before? Well, if you haven't, a play date is when mom or dad makes plans for someone to play with their child. On the other hand, if you have, you probably know what I know, you run out of ideas eventually! However, I have a few ideas for your next play date. Wouldn't it be great to plan a play date at the library where you could read to your child and his/her friend or friends? Another wonderful idea is to plan a game of "pretend" school. Where the parents get to be the teachers and the children get to be the students. Well, the rest is self-explanatory, and it's a great way to prepare toddlers for kindergarten, and the children in grades K or higher for next year's grade. You can also mix it up a bit, by switching roles. This is when the children get to play the teacher, and the parents of course get to be the students. Kids get a kick out of this kind of role-playing, and it's educational, too. Playing school give kids a chance to practice what they are learning in school such as writing, arithmetic, reading, letter recognition, and other things. It also gives the younger kids an idea what school is like. When they're pretending to be a student or a teacher, it gives you an opportunity to see your child in action. In many cases, they'll be imitating you or some other adult in their lives. It gives you the rare opportunity to see how your child imitates you, and if you like what you see, great, if not, you can always tweak yourself.

Another thing that is great about playing school is that your child is learning, as well as, having fun. Here are the basic instructions of the game (you may have to tweak them based on your child's age): You will need at least two players to play this game, dice, paper, jumbo pencils, and a pack of Brain Quest trivia cards. Next, throw the dice, whoever ends up with the highest number gets to be the teacher, and whoever ends up with the lowest number is the student. There can be more than one student but never more than one teacher. Of course, the game is more fun and competitive, if there is more than one student. The teacher in the game gets to ask questions from the deck of trivia cards. The student or students get to answer the questions. Five points are given for each correct answer, and twenty-five points for every genius question answered correctly. The student who gets 250 points first is the winner of the game. In addition, the students in the game should sit Indian style in front of the teacher. This will help simulate a real classroom setting.

So, as you can see play dates can be fun and educational, too! Well, what are you waiting for? Plan a play date today.

CHAPTER VIII

Dr. Seuss Books and The Things You Can Teach Your Child

Again, congratulations on choosing this book as a teaching tool to teach your child how to read and to give him/her a real head start in school. What's more, is that you are obviously determined to give your child the best head start in this race we call life. As the good book tells us, "…let us run with patience the race that is set before us, …" (*31. Heb. 12:1-3; http://bible.cc/hebrews/12-1.htm*) This is why it is important to teach our kids "how to" run the race. The race I'm talking about, isn't the kind of race where you come in first, by any means necessary (because some will cheat, lie, steal, and destroy to come in first), but the kind of race I'm referring to is the one you begin, and complete well with honesty. Diane Dew says that, "In any contest, the important factor is not how many begin the competition but who finishes the race and completes the course, who wins the prize. Late in life, Paul declared, "I have fought a good fight, I have finished my course, I have kept the faith." "… *there is in store for me the crown of righteousness… .* " *32. (2 Thessalonians 4:7-8) http://*

bible.cc/2_timothy/4-8.htm Scripture says we are to "run with patience (endurance, persistence) the race set before us, looking unto Jesus the Author and Finisher of our faith… For consider Him that endured…lest ye be wearied and faint in your minds." *33. (Heb 12: 1-3)." (Quoted from http://www.dianedew.com/runrace.htm).* Regardless of how smart our kids become, we really can't give our kids a "real" head start in school or in life, without also teaching them how to govern themselves according to the bible.

Therefore, I promise you this. If you keep reading to your child and insisting that he/she reads something new everyday, your child is going to get smarter and reach his/her full potential.

So, how is it going so far? Is your child enjoying learning how to read? Is he enjoying getting brighter? Are you enjoying the journey? Just stay in the moment and you will (if you aren't already)!

Another great thing you and your child can do is to become regulars at your local library or bookstore. I recommend buying or checking out a few Dr. Seuss books, because my children loved listening to these stories, and I know your children will, too. They loved these books for the quirky characters, funny interactions, and for the hilarious stories inside of these books. They also loved these books for all the shenanigans and rhyming text that was included in each book. The pictures are also colorful and very zany-like. I think your kids are going to love these books, too! How about starting a Dr. Seuss collection for your child (if you haven't already) with some of my children's favorites: 'The Cat in the Hat', 'The Cat in the Hat Comes Back' , 'Green Eggs and Ham', 'Horton Hears a Who!', 'Horton Hatches the Egg', and 'Oh, the Places You'll Go!'. These books are just bursting with all sorts of imagination and fun, and just waiting to be read by you!

In addition, when reading to your child, remember to read the story as if you are enjoying the story. I know this sounds simple enough, but for some parents it's not so easy. Reading children's books can take some getting used to, if you have not read one in a while. My husband reads children books quickly and every so often skips whole passages, and he even makes up his own endings sometimes! It's almost funny, but I would imagine that he is not the only one. On the other hand, our kids don't seem to mind so much that their dad is adding his own words. They're just happy their dad is reading to them, and your kids will like the way you read, too!

I strongly believe that reading to and with your child will become one of his/her favorite things to do, because it's one of our kids' favorite things to do, too. In the meantime, keep reading to your child and you are going to raise an incredible reader.

Additionally, always use your words to build your children up. What we say to our kids can help instill a great deal of confidence in them, if we use our words right. We all want our kids to feel special, and that we believe in them, right? So, let's start today lifting our kids up, not literally, but with our words.

As we build our kids up with words, let's not forget to build up their brainpower. On top of everything else, remember to embrace your kids' uniqueness, and help them grow into their God given talents.

Reading and learning new things as a family is a wonderful way for families to connect and grow closer. In the same way, it promotes communication among family members, including bickering siblings. Right now, we're living during a time where it seems like family members are going in a million directions. However, we must make learning a priority in our homes. Our children are depending on us to prepare them for their futures, whether they say it or not.

Another thing, we all know that equipping our kids with the ability to read before they start school is just smart. It's also a wise investment in our kids' schooling. Deciding what to read to our kids sometimes isn't always easy, because there are so many books to read. Besides, you can learn something from every book you pick up, but make sure you use reading time to teach your child something specific, like a new language. Books such as: "First Thousand Words in English" by Heather Amery, "My 1st Spanish Word Book: A Bilingual Word Book" by Angela Wilkes, and "The Usborne Book of Everyday Words in French" by Jo Litchfield, are all great books to introduce your child to a new language. All of these books can be purchased at www.amazon.com or check with your local library to see if they carry these books. Remember, we only get one chance to prepare our children for tomorrow's world (which I would imagine, will consist of many people speaking at least one different language). Therefore, it makes a lot of sense to teach our kids at least one foreign language.

So, as you teach your child different things, remember to keep all learning at home fun and light. You can do it! You can teach your child anything, if you put your mind to it. The sky's the limit!

I profoundly believe that one day our kids are going to grow up and thank us for teaching them how to read early and for giving them a "real" head start in school and in life. Yes, working with your kids at home is hard work, but all of our kids will have to make a living one day. So, let's help our kids succeed in school now, so that they can attend college, and choose the career of their choice in the future.

If your child could earn a full academic, sport, or music scholarship to attend college, would this inspire you to encourage your child do his/her best in school, sports, and in music lessons? Of course, it would. I know it would motivate me! Every parent in America would be thrilled if their child could earn a full scholarship to go to college, even the wealthiest of us. It would mean less money out of our pockets, right? Did you know that Georgia and 27 other states use all or some of its lottery earnings for public education according to research? *34. (http://sga.astate.edu/Documents/ EventsInfo/Lottery%20Research.pdf)* Also, allegedly more than 1 million Georgia students have attended college on lottery-funded hope scholarships since 1994 according to *35. (http://sga.astate.edu/Documents/EventsInfo/Lottery%20 Research.pdf).*

This is incredible, right? Programs like this one should motivate everyone to encourage their kids to do well in school, especially with college tuition on the rise. We have to make our kids smarter, so that they can qualify for scholarships like these and others.

"If you stay ready, you don't have to get ready", these are words of wisdom by Sheryl Lee Ralph. In other words, if your kids do well in school now, they won't have to get ready (or work so hard to get into a college) when they want to apply for a scholarship or for admittance into a college/ university. Therefore, going forward, let's take a stand on teaching our kids how to read early, along with some other things to give them a real head start in school.

It's important that we work with our kids at home, because I don't understand how a child can go to school for twelve whole years and no one discovers that he/she can't read. This is unbelievable to me! Yet, we have adults today, in our country who can't read. Can you explain this? You probably can't, but I know what we can do. We can make sure that adult illiteracy doesn't happen to our kids. We can prevent this from happening to our children, by teaching them how to read *early*, ourselves! So again, don't wait for someone else to teach your child how to read, add, subtract, or write. Every child should know these basics before beginning school.

Remember, what you teach your child is what he or she will grow up valuing. As it says in Proverbs, "Train up a child in the way he should go, and when he is old he will not depart from it," *(7. Proverbs 22:6 NIV)*. We must read to our children everyday and encourage them to read on their own, if they can. I cannot stress this enough, reading and learning has to be a priority in our homes, along with learning a musical instrument and playing at least, one or two sports year round.

As I am writing this, I am thinking about the fun time I will have later with my kids. I have an exciting evening planned filled with lots of books, educational videos on YouTube.com, bible DVDs, a few game boards, some healthy snacks, and a few throw pillows. To find educational videos on YouTube.com to view just go to www.youtube.com and search for anything educational you can think of for an example: conjunction function, Schoolhouse Rock Preamble, American history for kids, Book of Virtues, and so much more! Next, there's nothing to do, but enjoy each other's company and have some fun! The kids don't even realize their learning anything, either. It's a great way to spend quality time with your kids, as well as keep them smart. It's cool to learn new things together as a family, because a family that learns together stays smart together. Try planning a family night like this one with your kids! Don't forget to email us pictures with a quick note of all the fun! Who knows? Your entry may be chosen to appear on our website. So, start sending in those entries today at realheadstart@gmail.com!

I'm going to let you in on a little secret, just don't tell

anyone. I love reading to or with my kids and teaching them new things. Okay, this isn't a secret. I think you know this by now. I also enjoy watching how their eyes light up when they learn something new about the world that they didn't know before. It's just fascinating to me, and money can't buy it. Ponder this thought for just one moment. Our kids will not always live with us (I hope not-smile). One day they'll have families of their own, so, enjoy your kids while you have their *undivided* attention.

You can do all of this for your kids, too! Just set aside a little time each day to read and teach them something new. It's amazing how much you can learn in just about any book you can pick up or any story you read. Therefore, read to and with your kids as often as you can. You should definitely read books about other children, like Tom Sawyer in 'The Adventures of Tom Sawyer', Mary in 'The Secret Garden', and Roger in 'Thank You, M'am'. I believe children can learn a lot from books like these. It gives children perspective on how things used to be, and how to apply what the children learn in the stories to their own lives.

In addition, we're raising a generation of kids who think rising early to catch the early worm is so overrated. That is why I think it's a good idea to have our kids learn from the books like the ones I just mentioned and others. Besides, lessons learned back then, are still relevant today.

Don't forget to choose books about different topics like numbers, letters, manners, animals, fruits, countries, inventors, and just about anything, you can think of to introduce and teach your child about.

Bear in mind, the time you take each day to read to your child, is time well spent. When you read to your child, you are not only spending time with her, you are spending "quality" time with your child. By the way, don't forget to celebrate "National Kids Day" in August. "National

Kids Day, the American social phenomenon created by the 127-year-old national children's crisis charity Kids Peace, is encouraging adults to spend more meaningful time with the nation's children. This group is drawing phenomenal support from the American people, government groups, and a rapidly growing group of top child experts and advocates. National Kids Day has been recognized by the U.S. Congress, endorsed by the U.S. Conference of Mayors, and is now a rapidly growing social phenomenon with millions of participants involved in events at more than 10,000 locations since it was launched by Kids Peace in 1994." To find out more about this organization go to <u>www.kidspeace.org,</u> *(8. KidsPeace.org).*

Therefore, play games and watch different videos that are interesting with your kids, this way they'll have fun, and learn something, too! Keep in mind, what we consider "fun" sometimes, kids don't always agree. That's why it's important to keep everything playful, full of life, and entertaining, but knowledgeable, as well. It's also important to allow your child some free time after homework and any extra work you may give him/her at home. My kids love their free time or "me" time, because they get to spend it any way they like (within reason). When you mix learning with fun and free time, it's always a guarantee that your child will enjoy learning, and come back for more!

Remember, time set aside for reading or teaching your child how to read, is also a chance to teach him/her whatever you feel he/she needs to learn again or review. For instance, let's say your child just recently learned about Benjamin Franklin at school. It's a great idea to review what he has learned about Benjamin Franklin at home. A smart way to do this is to go to your local library, check out a book or video on Benjamin Franklin, and then discuss what the two of you just viewed or read. Another example, let's say your child needs to brush up on his/her manners a bit. Again, just go to the library, choose a fun book or video on manners, and discuss it afterwards. Let's say you want your child to learn more about the solar system. Then buy or check out a book on the solar system. You can even assist your child in making a replica of the solar system. All of this and more are the kind of things that help our children grow, dream, and become anything they want to become in the future.

Now, let's discuss an entirely different topic, teenage girls and boys. Let's say that your teenage son or daughter is going through puberty, and you are having a tough time talking to him/her about it. No problem, just go to your local library and check out "What's Happening to My Body (for boys)?" or "What's Happening to My Body (for girls)?" by Linda Madras. (You can also purchase these books on Amazon.com. Do not forget to tell your friends that they can purchase my book on Amazon.com, too.) In addition, reading this book with your child is a great way to spend more quality time with your teenager and answer any questions he/she may have. After reading and discussing the book, make the rest of the evening a movie night. Pick up a few snacks, your teenager's favorite movie (one you both can agree on), and watch it together. Now, you have just spent some "cool" quality time with your teenager. Who knew it would be this easy, right?

Take into account, your child is learning something every time you read to or with them, regardless of the subject. You are also helping your own brain stay healthy and sharp, when you teach your child new things.

Reading as a family, can be one of those traditions you pass down to your children. Just read different books together online and discuss what you read. It's like having a book club at home with your kids. A wonderful website to try is http://www.americanliterature.com/booktitleindex.

html; It's an unending supply of classic stories, the whole family can enjoy! Reading books and learning new things together can be both rewarding and fun for the entire family, as stated before. Now, that you are aware of some of the positive effects of reading together as a family, how about going to the website I just mentioned above and reading one of the stories today?

On a personal note, I am happy that my children treasure reading and learning at home. Sure, they like listening to music, watching television, playing video games, and sending messages via the cell phone like any other child. However, they also enjoy developing their talents, and learning just as much. That is why I am encouraging you to motivate your kids to learn something new or practice a sport, a foreign language, or a musical instrument a little everyday. Remember, what you do a little everyday adds up, and can be just as effective as any learning center.

I want my children to look back on their school days, and realize that mom and dad were right there. It isn't where you're educated, but where you're headed with what you've learned at school, at home, at church, and from the village -- that counts! Remind your kids to make the most of their education regardless of where they attend school. You should tell your kids that there are many professionals, sport stars, and celebrities in the world that attended public schools when they were children. Furthermore, tell your child that it isn't the school you attend that defines you, what does matter is taking the education you're given and using it to accomplish your goals.

I pray that all kids are blessed with parents like us, who are committed to making sure they do well in school. All parents can make a huge difference in what kind of education their kids receive at school, because all parents can make sure their kids are their best selves at school each day. They can also supplement their kid's education with the websites mentioned in the back of this book, resources available in their own communities, church, and online. If we help our kids succeed in school and in other activities, America's kids will be equipped to compete against all nationalities around the world. You see, in the future, we'll need the best in every field to keep America competitive, so let's give our kids the kind of training it's going to take for them to be extraordinary.

You can make reading time very special. Just choose a very quiet area in your home and make it as comfortable and as welcoming as you can. Here are a couple of things you can do to make your reading area cozy and inviting. All you have to do is add a couple of beanbags, a bright video game chair; a couple of big throw pillows, and some warm blankets and you've just created an inviting reading space in your own home. Complete the area by adding a small bookshelf, a colorful lamp, and some posters that encourage reading (you can buy these from any school supply store). Then, place a few books on top of the bookshelf that you know your kids will want to read, and ta-da, just like that, you've created a reading spot--like no other! Now, just read to and with your child as often as you can.

I read or heard it somewhere, that President Bill Clinton and First Lady Hillary Clinton were allegedly still reading to their daughter Chelsea Clinton at fourteen years old. Consequently, Chelsea Clinton went on to graduate from Stanford University. I guess all of that reading paid off. Well, it inspired me to do the same with my children, and family devotions are a great way to get the whole family to read (in addition to family night). A great book to try for family devotions is "Sticky Situations: 365 Devotions for Kids and Families" by Betsy Schmitt, and for more family devotions go to http://cbhministries.org/kfk/home.php.

Read to your child as often as you can, regardless of how old he/she is. You can read all sorts of books with and to your child, especially the ones that will teach him/her something he/she didn't know before. I don't read Dr. Seuss books with my fifteen year old anymore, or my eight year old. However, when Chelsea (my daughter) was thirteen years old, we read books together like: "The Care & Keeping of YOU" by American Girl, "A Smart Girl's Guide to Friendship Troubles", "A Smart Girl's Guide to Starting Middle School" (this book is also relevant for high school kids). At fifteen, we enjoy reading the "NLT Kids Bible" and "Sticky Situations" by Betsy Schmitt together. On the other hand, Joshua enjoys reading 'The Diary of a Wimpy Kid' series by Jeff Kinney, but I've also introduced him to some of the classics, like the ones, his dad and I enjoyed as children. Some of those classics (which I've mentioned before) are: 'Tom Sawyer', 'Oliver Twist', 'Anne of Green Gables', 'Tale of Two Cities', 'Pinocchio', 'The Secret Garden', and 'The Wizard of Oz'. I highly recommend these books for your children too, because they are timeless, thought provoking, and great vocabulary builders. Another great website to try that is excellent for building your child's vocabulary is www.wordlywise.com (click on students and press games to begin). As you know, having a great vocabulary (understanding the words you read) can help your child do well on tests. Therefore, mom and dad what are you waiting for, this is a great website for your child to try tonight.

I've probably mentioned this before, but some things are worth repeating. In my opinion, some things have to be repeated before they stick. At any rate, as you read to and with your child, remember to keep the story interesting and engaging. Read as if "you" want to find out what is going to happen next. For an example, when I read, I find myself just as curious about what is going to happen next in the story, as my kids are. That's the great part about being a parent; · you get to be a kid again (--enjoy it! I believe it keeps you young.).

Do you remember being a child and feeling carefree, with absolutely nothing to do? As a child, you probably felt like there was nothing in the world you couldn't do or accomplish, right? Well, now is your chance to relive some of those childhood memories. Just allow yourself to get into character when you are reading to or with your child. He/She will have a blast listening to you, too, and will come to love reading, which is exactly what we want him/her to do. Remember, "Children are an inheritance from the LORD. They are a reward from him." So, enjoy them, *(9. Psalm 127:3 God's Word Translation)*. To me, this bible verse reminds us to enjoy the gift of raising and teaching our kids. Let's also enjoy our kids' smiles, their laughter, and their love. More importantly, let's not forget to play with our children while you can, and teach them everything you know. The internet, textbooks, and the 100 plus websites in the back of this book can also help you educate your kids in a number of subjects. In addition, here are some great games to play with your children: 'peek-a-boo', which is a fun game for babies and toddlers, 'matching', and 'fish' are other great games for young children, but do not forget the old-fashioned games like 'store', 'catching', 'kick ball', and 'school' (as mentioned earlier). I will let you in on another secret, teaching your kids and playing with them, in my opinion, is the *real* fountain of youth.

Okay, I have talked enough, and you have read a lot about how to teach your child how to read and *why* it's important to teach him/her new things. Now, take a break and try putting some of these tips and suggestions into practice. Remember, the sooner you start, the quicker your child will learn to read and do other things.

I know it sounds too good to be true, but if you would just read to and with your child and teach him/her the alphabet, how to count, write, draw, and color before he/she starts school, he/she will automatically get a *real* head start. Additionally, singing pre-school songs along with your younger kids is an easy way to teach your child his/her letters, numbers, and how to count. All you have to do is encourage your child to sing along with you, when you pop in any of the following CDs: 'Alphabet Sounds: Songs That Teach' by various Artists, 'Favorite ABCs & Counting Songs' by Baby Genius, and 'Counting Songs' by Have Fun Teaching. Google all of the songs I just mentioned above on the internet to buy them. Next, make or buy big, colorful ABC's and numbers to place around your child's room or some other place in your home (as mentioned before), and point to the letters and numbers while you sing the songs together.

You really must make reading and learning precedence in your home, from this day forward. If you make education a priority in your home, I'm confident that your child will learn to read, get a *real* head start, and stay ahead, if you do. If you read to your child daily and encourage him/her to read on his/her own, you'll raise a bookworm. Some of the benefits of reading to and with your child often are the following: a bigger vocabulary, better test scores, and it's a wonderful way to teach your child something new. One way to encourage your child to read more is to buy books he/she loves to read. It doesn't really matter what your child is reading right now (as long as it's appropriate), but what's important is that he/she is reading and learning about new things.

Now, that you are fully on board and can see the point of reading to your child often, I have a question for you, "What are you going to read to or with your child tonight?" You should try reading something from http://www.edhelper. com . Edhelper.com is filled with an array of subject matter to read and teach your child. This website also has stories and questions (on every grade level) you can print off for your child to work on.

One day, we are going to expect our kids to know how to read anyway. That is why it's a good idea to teach your child how to read now. This is just the kind of dedication and commitment it is going to take for your child to get a real head start in school and in life.

As I've mentioned before, you should read to your child regularly. The more you read to your child, the smarter he/ she will become. It's just that simple. You've heard of this old saying before, and it has probably been told in a thousand different ways, yet the meaning is the same, "Talk is easy, but actually doing it, is another story."

So, let me tell you a story where I actually did something and didn't just talk about it. I have probably mentioned it before, but it's worth citing again. I read to both of my children before they were born, after they were born, and I still do (During family devotions and with them sometimes.). At any rate, before they were born, I would spend countless afternoons reading to both of my unborn babies. What did I read to a baby that wasn't even born yet? Well, that's a good question. I read every nursery rhyme book I could find. You are not going to believe this, but I could also feel my children moving in my womb when I was reading to them. I wasn't exactly sure what was happening, but I knew they were responding every time I read to them. Well, I later found out that they were responding to the sound of my voice, according to Terry Ross, an author and teaching activist I read about online--49. *http://ezinearticles. com/?Introducing-Your-Baby-To-Books-While-In-The-Womb-Isnt-As-Stupid-As-It-Sounds&id=305709.*

That is why you should begin reading to your baby while you are with child, because I believe it helps. After all, both of my kids were reading at the age of three, so I think that's proof that it does something. Whether or not you decide to read to your baby before he or she is born is up to you. I just feel like you have nothing to lose and everything to gain if you do. Well, if you don't read to your baby before he or she is born, you'll never know if it helped or not. On the other hand, if your baby is already here, congratulations (smile), and yes, you can read to a newborn baby or a toddler. By the way, if your child is in elementary school, middle school, or high school-- keep reading this book, because there's more in the book that is going to help your child soar in everything.

So, the fact that both of my kids were reading at three years old, along with some other things, is proof to me that children can learn many things *early*. If you are willing to put in the time and energy to teach your child, he/she can learn lots of things before he/she starts school. For instance, Terry Ross suggests that babies start learning language in the womb, and he goes on to say that a baby learns to recognize his/her mother's voice from all other voices. He believes babies trust and recognize their mother's voice outside of the womb, for this reason. He also believes children learn the language, they hear the most. Terry believes mothers can teach their children how to read and help them associate objects to words, if they read and communicate often with their baby. *(10. Introducing Your Baby to Books While In the Womb Isn't As Stupid As It Sounds by Terry Ross:* http://ezinearticles.com)

This doesn't suggest that the baby couldn't recognize the father's voice; it just means that the baby will be more familiar with the voice it hears the most. Keep in mind, the baby is around the mother more anyway, for obvious reasons. It's a good idea to have the father read to the unborn baby, so that he or she will be familiar with the father's voice, also.

It's okay if you find yourself reading the same books repeatedly. Besides, repetition is a wonderful tool to use when teaching your child how to read. It is also a great way to help your older children excel in school. Just don't forget to go over their homework, and to check for any errors to make sure they understand everything.

When teaching toddlers how to read, write, color, draw, count, add, etc. at home, find a quiet space where your child can learn. This space should be well lit, neat, and stocked with school supplies. If they are younger, why not add a home library and a make shift pre-school? All you would have to do is add a teacher and child's desk, a make believe kitchen, house, and theatre stage (To act out plays from both of these websites http://www.storiestogrowby.com/script.html and http://www.storiestogrowby.com/script.html.). Next, use your imagination, the way the fictional character Barney tm does, and use markers to draw big colorful and fun pictures on very large boxes to create anything you want. You should also invite your kids to help you make some of the props for the make believe school. Boxes can be turned into tents, pretend houses, and almost anything, you and your child can think of. By the way, don't go out and buy anything new. You should shop at garage sales and thrift shops for the desks, pretend kitchen, and some of the other things mentioned (don't forget to wash them down with a little 409). Then, all you have to do is invite a few of your child's friends over and watch the games begin! Don't forget to let them watch videos like these before they start to play (since, it is important for children to imitate positive dialogue and imagery): "The Berenstain Bears-Discover School" and "The Berenstain Bears-Visit the Dentist".

It's also a known fact that children learn when they play pretend or imitate their favorite role models--you of course, their teacher, their favorite "positive" sports star or celebrity, or grandma and grandpa. That is why it's important that we monitor what our children view on television, movies, and our own "reality shows at home" (not the reality shows on TV, but how we behave at home). If our kids have positive role models to imitate, it can help them reach their full potentials. It can also help our kids grow and stretch, as well. Besides, when children role-play, they also get to problem solve and make important decisions that they don't usually get to make on their own. Therefore, encourage your kids to think and solve problems for themselves when they role-play.

Don't forget to play classical music softly in the background while your child is playing or while you are teaching your child. Since, kids naturally blossom in environments where there's classical music playing, books to read, and props to explore.

In addition, parents' attitude about their kids' education and their kids' teachers, usually determine how their kids perform in school. When parents encourage and insist their kids respect their teachers and listen in class everyday, kids typically do better in school.

A lot of you may feel it's too early to read to or start teaching your younger kids how to read. That's why I'm suggesting you read the entire collection of Dr. Seuss books to your toddlers, because if you read them right (with lots of expression) your kids are going to love listening to these stories. They are fun books that keep kids interested and captivated. In addition, these books have an unbelievable way of capturing the hearts of youngsters everywhere. Therefore, read all kinds of books to your kids, but make sure you include Dr. Seuss books, too. Oh my, the things your kids are going to learn!

Reading to your child instinctively teaches him/her new things. Therefore, read everyday to your child. Read to him/her while traveling, running errands, or while you are at the doctor's office. Point out and read billboards to your child, cereal boxes, happy meal bags, recipes, magazines, books, short stories, and the newspaper. What's important is you are reading to your child daily, and that he/she is learning something.

By the way, you are going to have so much fun reading different books to your child and helping him/her get smarter. I can remember reading books about lions, tigers, and bears, "Oh, my!" Each one seemed more magical than the last. I also remember playing lots of classical music before naps and in the evenings before bedtime. As they grew older, I played games with them like matching, Monopoly™, Life™, and other games that encouraged fun and learning. Activities like these and others foster learning, reading, and can inspire your child to learn more.

Nevertheless, keep in mind, your child will not learn how to read overnight. Yet, every book you read, every song you encourage your child to sing, every word you point out, will put him/her one-step closer to reading on his/her own one day.

As you continue to teach your child how to read, don't forget to read as if you are one of the characters in the story, as I've mentioned many times before. You will retain your child's attention better if you do, and he/she will learn more. In addition, if your child is reading already, try reading the story together. If you read the story in an exciting way, more than likely your child will read the story in the same way. You don't have to be perfect. Just be yourself and pretend you're acting like the character would. Let the punctuation marks and words guide you as you read to and with your child. For an example, in this sentence, "I will certainly help you, ma'am, for a slice of your homemade apple pie. I'm starved!" The author clearly wants the reader to know that this character is hungry and excited about helping the woman, because he can't wait to eat a slice of her homemade apple pie. Therefore, the sentence above should be read with lots of eagerness and excitement in your voice. Just think how you would read the sentence above if you were trying out for a part in a play. You probably would read the sentence with a whole lot of enthusiasm and feeling, right? That is why you must tell your child to obey the rules of punctuation marks, so that he/she will read like the author intended his/her readers to do. You should also lead by example when you read. Your child has probably heard many readers read in many different reading voices. He/She may have also noticed how some of the readers' voices seemed to rise and fall when they read. When your voice changes in tone or pitch, it is called inflection. We should read as if we are in the moment (in the story so to speak), and change our voices as the characters' moods changes. Just think about it, a story just sound more interesting when the reader changes his/her pitch or tone throughout the story. This style of reading makes the story more upbeat and it just flows better. It's almost like listening to a play or a movie by radio.

Try using different voices for each character when you read to your child. It helps bring the story to life. Your child will also learn to read stories like you, so remember to make a good impression when you're reading to him/her or with him/her. He will listen and notice how your voice goes up for question marks and exclamation points, how it stops and pauses at periods and commas, and how it gets soft or rumbling for different characters throughout the story. In addition, your child will learn best, by how you read to him, not by what you tell him. Does this sound familiar? Do as I say, not what I do? Well, this doesn't work in reading. Your child is prone to read exactly how you read to him/her. So, make sure you are reading stories the way you want him/her to read.

Reading to your child as often as you can, or having someone read to him/her when you can't do it, in my opinion, will make your child smarter. You should even ask grandma and grandpa to read to your child when he/she goes over for a visit. If your child attends a daycare center, check to make sure that they are reading several times throughout the day, as well. Overall, the goal here is to make sure your child is being read to everyday.

If your baby or toddler is read to several times during a day, I believe, your child will learn to read by the age of three or right before he/she turns four. This is a real possibility, because I read to my children all the time, and they both were reading at three years old. I read to Chelsea and Joshua before they were born, after they were born and almost everyday after that, and when they were three, they both were reading to me. They just sort of plopped down by me one day, opened one of their favorite books at the time (maybe one of the My First I Can Read Books Biscuit series by Alyssa Satin Capucilli) and just started reading. That is what I envision for you. That one day when you least expect it, your child is going to sit right next to you and start reading to you, too. You'll see! Just keep reading those Dr. Seuss books with lots of inflection and in a fun and zany like way, and your child will be reading in no time (if he/she isn't reading already). It may take 36 months (or less) or up to 48 months or more before your child learns to read, but regardless of when he/she learns, it will certainly be worth the wait.

So, please read often at home, and it's also a good idea for your children to "see" you reading, as well, because when a child reads or is read to, it expands his/her view of the world and opens his/her eyes to the possibilities that are out there. You can start today, by reading the newspaper, a magazine on your iPad, a news story on the internet, or your favorite book. You can also start a "DEAR" time in your home, and it means to drop everything and read. Each letter stands for something. The D stands for drop, the E stands for everything, the A stands for 'and', and the R stands for read. You can even read to the neighborhood children when they come over to play. You can also encourage the children to read a book before they start to play. Make sure the reading area (the one we talked about earlier) is inviting, and filled with interesting and exciting books.

By the way, if you don't get a chance to read to your child every single day, don't worry about it. Some days, you'll get the chance to read to your child a lot and then some days you won't. That's okay, because what counts is what you do *most* of the time. Just keep reading to your child as much as you can. I understand that as parents, we all have other responsibilities and titles like boss, employee, entrepreneur, wife, husband, son, daughter, sister, brother, aunt, uncle, neighbor, friend, and volunteer. Therefore, that is why I say read as often as you can to your child, when you can, because even reading once a day at bedtime can make a world of difference. However, if your child is a reader, encourage him/her to read on his/her own. Why not, it gives you a chance to close your eyes and just listen. Aaaaaah!

You can never teach your kids too much. Therefore, to teach your kids something new, just introduce them to it, in a number of different ways. For example, if you want to teach your children about Helen Keller read a book about her and then show them The Animated Story of Helen Keller Video on Interactive DVD by Dove. This video can be purchased at   http://www.nestlearning.com/the-animated-story-of-helen-keller-video-on-interactive-dvd_p42844.aspx. If there happens to be a play in town about Helen Keller, take them to see it. It's another great way to make sure your kids learn more about Helen Keller and multiple exposures will help your kids remember her.

Again, if you don't get to read or teach your child something new everyday, that's okay. Remember, the important thing is what you do "most" of the time, as I mentioned before, not what you do some of the time. What you do most of the time, usually sticks anyway. That is why it is critical to make an effort to read to your child most days, so that when you can't do it, it won't be a big deal. It's just like exercising. If you exercise at least five days a week, and can't for a couple of days for whatever reason, it's no big deal, just as long as you get back to your normal exercise routine. As I said before, what really matters is what we do *most* of the time.

Therefore, always work with your kids at home, by teaching them how to read, as well as, something he/she may not know, yet. You should also continue reading to and with your kids, because it's a great way for your child to learn about the world he/she lives in. By the way, don't forget to have your child work on the different websites mentioned in this book, to give him/her a real head start in school.

CHAPTER IX

Classical Music as a Learning Tool & Other Teaching Methods

Another thing I am going to suggest is that you play classical music for your child as often as you can. "Just as it's vitally important to eat good-quality food right from the start, so we are deeply affected by the music we hear from a very early age, even in the womb," Peter Kindersley says." *(11. "Does classical music make babies smarter?" By Denise Winterman BBC News Magazine)*

Play classical music everywhere! Play it in the car, at naptime, in the evenings, because I believe classical music can help kids become smarter. In my opinion, classical music is one of the reasons my kids are smart today. Why? Well, I played it all the time for my kids when they were younger, and they have performed well in school, ever since. I played classical music for my kids before they were born, when they were babies and toddlers, in pre-school, in kindergarten, and in elementary school (I still play it occasionally for Joshua.). You should also play it for your children. Play classical music when your kids are doing their homework, working on a school project, or just for fun. I believe classical music made all the difference in the way my kids interpret data today. It probably made it easier for them to learn to read. Well, what are you waiting for? Turn on the Ipod or CD player and play some classical music for your kids!

Many believe exposing your child to positive tunes like classical music can also help your child become an exceptional student in school. Don't forget to expose him/her to good media, too. When I say "good" media, I mean G rated movies, plays, videos, and television programming for the entire family. 'G' stands for *good*, right? No, it actually means according to the ratings board's opinion there's nothing in the film that *might* be offensive to parents. Yet, the film may still contain an inappropriate word like "heck" and some violence as reported on 36. http://www.associatedcontent.com/article/738155/movie_ratings_meanings_for_parents.html . Therefore, it is really up to us to shield our kids from the wiles of this world. It should always be our goal to familiarize our children to wholesome and new things that will help them grow and learn. Exposing your younger kids to quality things like: classical music, pre-school songs, educational games, fun children plays, and reading books about "Madeline" and "Junie B. Jones", will help give them the kind of head start every parent wants for their kids.

The beginning phase of a child's life *should* include classical music. Professor Paul Robertson has said, and I quote, "There is compelling scientific evidence that the music, we hear at the earliest ages significantly affect the way our neurological pathways are laid down during development." *(12. www.musicmindspirit.org, quoted on http://www.itummy.net/references.php)*

The best classical music to play in my opinion is Mozart, Beethoven, Handel, and Chopin. You may want to start with a couple of CDs that has a combination of classical composers like "Build Your Baby's Brain" and "Baby Einstein" by Lullaby Classics. These CDs can be purchased at www.amazon.com. It's a good idea to play these CDs for your baby and toddler anytime of the day. When your child turns about six years old, update his/her classical music collection with these classical tunes: "World's Very Best Opera for Kids Music in English!", "Classics for the Kids", and "Beethoven's Wig: Sing along Symphonies".

Did you know that researchers have said they believe babies begin to hear in the womb at around 15 weeks? *(13.* http://www.askamum.co.uk/Pregnancy/Search-Results/ Week-by-week/How-is-your-baby-developing-in-the-womb/). This proves to me that playing classical music while you are with child is a smart thing to do for your unborn baby. I started playing classical music for my unborn baby, when I was around 7 1/2 months pregnant, and she moved every time I played it for her. Therefore, I concur that babies can hear in the womb. At any rate, playing classical music when you are at least 15 weeks, sounds like a good idea to me.

So, what do you think? Does it sound like a good idea to you? I hope so, because I truly believe classical music can make babies smarter. I think it has something to do with how our brains interpret the music. Even so, whether it works or not, what harm can it do if we play it for our kids?

My point is this. The effects of classical music on children's learning can be significant for some and not so significant for others. Whether or not classical music makes your child smarter or not, really boils down to a matter of opinion. Yet, I believe it can be a valuable teaching tool.

Furthermore, "studies suggest that playing classical music for your baby, while they are still in the womb and during a baby's formative years, builds neural bridges that are responsible for carrying information in the brain. Additionally, classical music can stimulate the alpha waves in the brain, and calm and soothe young children", according to research done by Indiana.edu. *(15. Indiana. edu: Human Intelligence Mozart Effect* www.indiana. edu/~intell/mozarteffect2.shtml*)*. To me, this proves that classical music has some kind of effect on babies and young children, and as mentioned before, some aren't sure what that effect is. Nevertheless, we all can agree on one thing, and that is classical music can be effective, in some way or the other. For instance, some pre-schools and elementary schools play classical music, because they believe it can make their students smarter. I was also inspired to play classical music at my learning center, since I was already playing it for my daughter. Classical music has been so effective that hospitals have been inspired to give out free classical CDs to all mothers. They are hoping that the mothers will play it at home to calm, soothe, and perhaps help their babies get smarter. I was one of those parents who went home with a classical CD from the hospital, just to add to the other ones I was already playing at home. I agree that classical music can calm, soothe, and yes make your baby smarter.

Keep in mind that I did not play the CD once or twice, and in my opinion, my baby was smarter. I actually played it over and over again. I believe introducing kids to something several times or more when teaching them something new; can help them learn it better. When you play it for your baby, remember to play it softly for him/her. Playing music too loudly may hurt your baby's ears. Many parents today are embracing this idea and are exposing their children to classical music as often as they can. So, have I convinced you to try it? I sure hope so.

In addition to reading to your kids and playing classical music for them, you should also teach them *how to* read, write, and do arithmetic. Teaching your kids these skills before they start kindergarten, will help prepare them for school and give them a *real* head start.

Don't you think it's a great idea to teach your child how to read, along with learning how to write, and do math before he/she starts kindergarten? Of course, it is. Who wouldn't want their child to learn to read, write and do math before starting school? Well, all you have to do is follow the five easy steps in this book, along with some other suggestions and tips and your child will be on his/her way to learning how to read and more!

Make sure you review with your child at home what he/she is learning at school, to keep him/her ahead. Furthermore, you must constantly introduce him/her to new concepts and ideas throughout the school year to keep him/her smart. Whew! That sounds like a lot, but it's worth it! I should know! Joshua made all A's on his third grade report card for the first semester dated 02/11. I am so happy for him. He worked hard for these grades, and I made sure he did!

Let me say this before I move on. Parents you can't wait until the report card comes home to see how your child is doing in school. Make it your business to know what is going on at school each day or at least each week. In other words, know all tests dates and make sure your kids prepare for them by listening in class, doing all of their homework, and studying what he/she has learned in class. We can only ask our kids to do their best, right? Well, that means that *our kids* can make at least all A's and B's on their report card… after all, *they're our kids*. We can't give our kids crutches to stand on, if we do, they might lean on them. In other words, our kids are bright and capable, and they can do whatever they makeup their minds to do. Don't give them an excuse to perform below their capabilities, mom and dad.

By the way, you are going to be so happy when your

child learns how to read. If your child is in kindergarten or in a higher grade and isn't reading yet, that's okay, just continue working with him/her until he/she does. I believe every child has the capability to learn how to read early, if someone takes the time to teach him/her.

Just spend a few minutes each day teaching your child the methods in this book and your child will be reading in no time. All you have to do is make the commitment to invest the time necessary to teach your child how to read, and I promise you that your child will learn to read. After all, the reading methods I am sharing with you in this book are the same ones I used to teach my kids how to read.

The techniques in this book *are* effective, because they worked with my own children, and I'm confident that they will work with your kids, too.

Remember, that your child will naturally respond to non-stop love, praise, encouragement, reading, singing, playtime, classical music, flash cards, and other methods referred to in this book. You'll be having so much fun with your child that it won't even feel like you're teaching him/her anything.

As I stated before, it is not necessary to rush the five reading steps mentioned in this book. Move on to the next step when your child has mastered the step before it. Keep in mind, every child learns differently and at his/her own pace. Our job is to work with our kids, so that they will reach their full potentials. For an example, if your child answers a double-digit addition problem wrong, ask him/her to solve it again while you watch him/her do it. It may be that he/she forgot to carry the number and add it to the other numbers in the other column. Sometimes it's just that simple. Making sure your child understands why he/she didn't get a problem right can make a world of difference on upcoming quizzes and tests. If you can't help your children do their homework, that's okay. Have your child complete the problems he/she can. Then, remind him/her to ask his/her teacher about them the next day in class or call this homework helpline 1-800-866-BIGY at *50.http://*www.bigy.com/education/hwhl.php during the hours 4:00 pm - 7:00 pm or Google™ "homework helpline" for others.

Keep in mind, when working with your child at home, try not to think about what you have to do later or what went on earlier that day (kids can tell if you are fully paying attention to them or not). Nothing matters right now. What's important is that you are there for your child when he/she needs you. In addition, you must make sure your child work on one of the websites mentioned in this book at least 30 minutes a day to keep him/her smart. Just think about it, do you really want to waste the time you've invested in giving your child a real head start, by not continuing to work with him/her at home? Do you want him/her to lose his/her advantage? Of course, you don't. That is why you have to work with him/her in grades kindergarten through 12th grade. That might mean reminding him/her to do his homework, dropping him/her off at the library to study, encouraging him/her to study for tests and quizzes, and insisting that he/she manages his/her time effectively.

Your child is learning many things for the first time, and it's up to you to make sure he/she is retaining what he/she is learning at school. It is your responsibility to make sure your child learns in school, so that he/she won't be locked out of the American dream. You must motivate your child to go after his/her goals with all of his/her might, as if the whole world was cheering him/her on. In addition, remind him/her that sometimes you have to put in extra time or lose a little sleep to accomplish your goals. Remind your kids to apply themselves in school, so that they will have a better chance at achieving their goals in the future.

Remember, kids are a lot smarter than we think they are, as I have stated before. Therefore, try this technique at home with your three and four year olds who have completed the five reading steps in this book. Choose your child's favorite book and read it to him twenty eight times, while pointing to words and pictures every time you read it. Don't try reading it 28 times in one day or over several days, but read it at least once a day for 28 days. It takes about 28 days for something to become a habit. So, if it takes you two to three months to read your child's favorite book 28 times, that's perfectly okay. After you have read it to your child at least twenty eight times over a good amount of time, see if he/she can read it on his/her own. Your child may read it right away and then again, he/she may not. If your child can read the book all by himself/herself, congratulations, but if he/she can't, that's okay, too. Just continue working with your child at home, until he/she does.

Kids are like sponges. They soak up knowledge, like a sponge soaks up water. So, teach them as much as you can. Don't underestimate what they can learn. Just remember to show lots of enthusiasm when teaching your kids different things, because it will help your children pay attention more. If you keep reading and singing to your child, not only will he/she learn to read, he/she will also get a head start on learning other things. All of your time, talent, and energy that you're investing in your child will pay off one day. I'm confident it will. It certainly paid off for this family according to 19 Action News *37.* http://www.19actionnews. com/Global/story.asp?S=13865892&clienttype=printabl e, when their three-year-old son saved their lives from a fire. The local fire station rewarded the little boy for his courageous act of saving his family. The little boy learned in pre-school what to do in case of a fire. Therefore, this proves that kids can learn and do great things at any age, if we teach them. Therefore, teach and work with your child at home, so that he/she will reach his/her full potential in life.

Many parents feel like school is responsible for teaching their kids how to read. I disagree with this kind of thinking, as I've stated before. We shouldn't wait for others to teach our kids anything. The alarming illiteracy rates in the United States should be enough to motivate every parent to teach their kids how to read early. Were you even aware of the adult illiteracy statistics in America? I think most people are aware of the problem, but just don't think it will ever happen to them or to anyone they know. Nevertheless, many individuals suffer from this epidemic every year, and no one can really pinpoint why some adults attended school for 13 years and didn't learn to read. This is why I am encouraging you to teach your own children how to read early, along with other things like arithmetic, writing, and memorization. If we teach and work with our kids at home, we can decrease their chances of becoming a statistic.

Teaching kids new things is easy to do, because believe it or not-- they naturally want to learn. After you teach your kids how to read, make sure you teach him/her other skills that will give him/her a head start in school. The sky is the limit what you can teach your kids at home to give them a head start and to keep them ahead. I believe children who live in homes where education is stressed, taught, and valued, simply apply themselves in school more.

Do you *still* think it is too early to teach your toddler how to read? Well, I hope you think it's a great idea now, after learning about the alarming illiteracy rates in our country. With all the talk these days about raising academic standards, as an effort to give our kids a quality education, it amazes me why anyone would question teaching our kids anything before they start kindergarten. Kids are born ready to learn, so teach them. Bear in mind, that when you teach your kids something like how to solve division problems, before they learn it in school; you increase their chances of excelling at division.

It is the opinion of some, that a great deal of our kids aren't receiving a quality education these days, while others are. They are afraid that the children, who aren't receiving a quality education, will be left behind. There are many who would like to see *every* child in America get a quality education, and we all can help. One way we can help is to teach our kids how to read, write, and do basic arithmetic before they go to school. This kind of preparation would give our kids a *real* head start in school and put them on the right track to getting a quality education. I know we can do this for our children, because I'm doing it for my kids, and so can you. I must be honest, though. It takes a lot of work to look over your child's homework everyday, and to make sure he/she is prepared for most quizzes and tests. Sometimes, you'll feel like your own children are working against you. Yet, don't give up! We have to give our kids the kind of head start that will help them succeed in school now and in the future, later.

Sometimes we have to be the change we want to see. We have to make sure that our kids are well read and knowledgeable about different things. We have to send them to school knowing something new everyday. We can use the internet to teach our kids all sorts of things everyday (like from the 100+ websites in the back of this book), if we take the time to do it. Well, you may not get around to doing it every single day, but try to do it at least five times a week. Is that too much to ask? We have to teach our kids new things, as well as encourage them to work towards making better grades in school. If we can't do it, then we *must* find a learning center that can.

If your child knows how to read already, that's excellent! Just remember to teach him/her something he/she hasn't learned already. Think about it. Everyday is another opportunity to equip our kids with the kind of skills that it's going to take to be competitive in the future. In addition, we must raise our kids to be contributing members of society. By working with our children at home and exposing them to knowledge ahead of time, can help increase our kids' chances of succeeding in life. All we have to do is make it a priority to teach our own children how to read early, along with teaching them other basic learning skills like addition and subtraction, writing, drawing, coloring, shapes, a foreign language, a musical instrument or how to play their favorite sport.

Teaching and learning is a never-ending cycle, so to speak. We can always teach and expose our kids to something new. Let's not wait and see how our kids are going to do in school. We must be active in our kids' education from day one. One of the ways we can do this is by emailing the teachers and asking the right questions that will help our kids do well in school. You can also remind your children to do their homework everyday, study for all tests and quizzes and turn in their school projects on time.

I think today's kids have many distractions, and they need you mom and dad to help them navigate around them. You probably are wondering, what distractions? I mentioned some of them earlier, but in addition to those: movies, television, commercials, video games, and the internet. Many companies are aggressively targeting (in my opinion) 13 to 17 year olds to get on face book, to get a cell phone, an iPad, a Wii, an Xbox, an iPod, a digital camera, etc.. If I were a teenager, it would be hard for me to concentrate if I had all of these! That is why we must remind our kids to do their best in school every single day. It's also a good idea to make sure your child reads assigned chapters and the chapter assessment that goes with every chapter before every test. Lastly, make sure your child attends school each day and arrives on time. In order to accomplish this, make sure your child go to bed at a good time and have a nutritious breakfast in the morning. Good attendance can make a world of difference in your child's performance at school.

I believe there is a silent war going on (as cited before), and we have to help our children win by encouraging our kids to read and learn more. Yes, balance learning with fun, but always encourage your child to read and learn new things. We have to teach our kids math and science skills that will give them an edge in school. Here's an excellent resource you can start using right now that will help your child learn geography better, and it's free-- go to http://weeklyreader.com/kids/games/geography.asp ._For other educational games like this, go to http://www.weeklyreader.com/wr/6.

Now, let's get back to my point on why we all should make it a priority to help our kids get a quality education. We shouldn't have to lean on school lotteries, praying that our child's number is selected, so that he/she will get a chance to attend a charter school that "promises" a quality education. We shouldn't have to send our kids to private school, just because we *think* they'll get a better education, if we do. We shouldn't have to use someone else's address, so that our kids can go to another school we *think* is better than the one being offered in our own neighborhoods. Our kids do not have to go to certain schools to get a quality education. We can help our kids get a quality education, by making sure, they go to school each day *on time* and *prepared*. Another thing we can do is to insist that they *sit up front* and *listen to their teachers*, so that they can learn what the teacher is *trying* to teach them. We can also *supplement their education* at home, by having them work on the websites mentioned in the back of this book. Besides, in my opinion, it doesn't matter what school a child attends, *if he/she doesn't apply himself/herself,* whether he/she attends a charter, public, home, online, or private school, he/she may still find himself/herself left behind.

We have to stop thinking about what we don't have, and focus more on what we do have, in America. In other words, let us be thankful for the schools we do have, because there are many countries that do not have an education system in place or fresh water for their citizens to drink. We are so blessed to live in a country where we have schools, free air-conditioned libraries with all kinds of books, and many other educational resources. The change we want to see, as I've said before has to begin with us and in our own homes. We have to take the initiative and use the free educational resources that we have available to us. We must also educate ourselves on ways that we can help our children learn more, in addition to, what they are learning in school. Your child should always be in the process of learning new things, regardless of what school he/she attends.

We must always encourage our kids to listen and pay attention in school, so that they'll learn something. I believe all kids can receive a quality education from any school in America, if they are motivated enough to. We have to encourage our kids to give a 100% in school and in extra-curricular activities. Extra-curricular activities like sports, music, gymnastics, dance, drama, and cheerleading. They can help your child develop his/her talents and increase his/her confidence level. You should "expect" your child to do excellent in school, as well as, give him/her the resources to help him/her do it. At some point (maybe by 6th grade--if not sooner) your child should also begin expecting more from himself/herself. You should always remind your child to do his/her best in school, so that he/she can achieve his/her goals in the future.

Good grades are an indication that your child is learning in school, and they can help him/her do well on tests. Therefore, we have to encourage our kids to listen and participate in class more, so that they will learn their lessons. Some children are motivated enough to listen and pay attention on their own, while others may not be as motivated. As mentioned before, keep your kids on track, so that they'll learn the skills necessary to be competitive in the future. It's true that some kids are self-motivated, as in this example. I remember one day, giving one of my daughter's orchestra classmates a compliment for doing extremely well in orchestra class, and she replied, "I'm only doing what is expected of me." I thought to myself, "What an excellent student." Let's encourage our kids to do what is expected of them, too, by expecting them to do well in school.

Nowadays, I believe every child can get a quality education, if he/she applies himself/herself in school. We are fortunate to be living during a time where information and knowledge is available at our fingertips. So, what does that mean to you and me? Well, it means we can use the information and knowledge available on the internet to help supplement (enhance, add to, fill out, improve, complement) our kids' education. In addition, we must see to it that our kids attend school each day, as well as do all of their class work and homework, in a timely manner.

Let's consider President Abraham Lincoln for a moment. When Abraham Lincoln was a boy, all he wanted to do was read. He read every book he could get his hands on. Ultimately, he gave himself an adequate education. Then, he read everything he could about the law, and eventually earned his law degree. He eventually became the President of the United States! "Wow!" "Unbelievable!" It just goes to show you, if a person really wants a quality education in America, all he/she has to do is apply himself/herself. If

Abraham Lincoln were alive today, he would probably be in the library reading, now.

So, let's do what is necessary to keep our kids on the road to success. Our kids are up for the challenge. Our job is to keep them focused and inspired. I know you are eager and motivated to do your part, because really who wants their kids to be left behind? I would suspect that no one does! We all have the power to make it happen for our kids, and I trust we all will.

Do not let Facebook, Myspace, Twitter, You Tube, iPods, television and cell phones become a distraction or an obstacle for your child. We have to find a way to help our children manage their time effectively and around these diversions. We have to see to it that our kids reach their full potentials. That might mean hiring a tutor, asking a family member or friend for help, or simply helping your child yourself.

In addition to making our kids smart, we must teach our kids to be responsible, to respect their elders and peers, and to mind their manners. Remind your kids often of this bible verse from Luke 6:31, which says, "Do to others as you would have them do to you." *38. NIV©1984* http://bible. cc/luke/6-31.htm, maybe it will remind them to get along with others and respect their teachers. It's also a good idea to have them read biographies of accomplished individuals, so that they can learn from their lives.

I believe if everyone would go out and buy this book for every parent he/she knows, we'll win this war on education in America, one child at a time. We have to do it for our kids, and for our country. America in my opinion is number one. One way we can keep America a beacon on a hill and resilient is to make sure that our kids get a quality education. Every child in America can potentially become one of America's future leaders, presidents, politicians, teachers,

Pharmaceutical business professionals, entrepreneurs, authors, owners, astronauts, scientists, and inventors. This is why we must make sure that every child in America receives a quality education, because if one child's right to a quality education is threaten, it can be a threat to every child (An idea I got from listening to President John F. Kennedy address to the Nation on Civil Rights-June 11, 1963), 52. http://www.youtube.com/watch?v=vitqaJ7VKqQ&feature=related. I am asking everyone in America to change the dialogue, and let's all encourage the children in our lives and the ones we see out and about to do their best in school. Let's reward our kids for doing well in school, because it is a step in the right direction to get our kids excited about excelling in school again. We have to encourage our kids to graduate from high school on time and to go on to college. The more our kids learn the better our country will be. Then, we'll be in a position to compete around the world and win this war on education. We have to help our children achieve the new American dream, "a quality education", by encouraging, challenging, and motivating them everyday.

If you teach your child how to read early, you won't have to worry about them becoming a statistic one day, as stated before. That's another reason why it is important to work with your child at home to make sure they are learning all the lessons that are being taught at school and more. The more your child learns, the more he'll/she'll know, and the more he/she knows, the more he'll/she'll earn in the future.

I hope I have inspired you to become more involved in your child's education. This quote from National Adult Literacy (as briefly mentioned before) should motivate you even more. "According to the National Adult Literacy Survey, 42 million adult Americans can't read; 50 million can recognize so few printed words they are limited to a 4th or 5th grade reading level; one out of every four teenagers drops out of high school, and of those who graduate, one out of every four has the equivalent or less of an eighth grade education." *(16. The National Right to Read Foundation).* This statistic should inspire everyone to teach their children how to read early and make sure they learn on their grade level in grades kindergarten through 12th grade. Visit this website *http://www.nrrf.org/essay_Illiteracy.html* and read for yourself the daunting research on illiteracy in our country.

You should also help your child increase his/her vocabulary, so that he/she can do well on standardized tests. Have him/her work on www.wordlywise.com (Sign up to get a 30 day free trial) to build his/her vocabulary. Kids who are taught things before they learn them in school, are more confident in class, oppose to learning things for the first time. So, let's introduce and teach our kids different things at home, to give them a great head start in school. Our kids will continue to do well, if the same kind of determination that went into giving them a "real" head start in the first place, goes into keeping them ahead. Consistency is the key to keeping your child ahead. So, continue teaching your child at home and encouraging him/her to do well in school.

We all can help our children become better students, because we can insist that they do their homework everyday with the television off, and give them extra schoolwork to complete at home to keep them smart. Volunteering at your child's school is also a great way to become involved in your child's education. It shows him/her you care. You should also communicate with your child's teacher on a regular basis to make sure your child stays on course. In addition to doing all of this, you can also become a part of the PTA, attend meetings, and lend a hand where needed.

Although, volunteering at your child's school is commendable, I can't stress enough how important it is to make sure your child is doing well in school. Reviewing with him/her at home and going over homework together is a great way to make sure he/she understands what he/she is learning in school. You should also teach your child new things at home (as I've mentioned before), to keep him/her smart and ahead.

You won't believe this, but some kids graduate from kindergarten without learning how to read. Can you even imagine sitting in class all year long not fully understanding what the teacher was writing on the board or being able to understand the directions on a worksheet? It isn't the kids' fault, either. So, whose fault is it? Is it their parents' fault or is it the teachers' fault? One may argue that it is the teachers' fault, but on the other hand, one may argue that it is the parents' fault. Well, this is what I think. I think the time that is being invested to figure out whose fault it is, should be used to teach the kids how to read. Therefore, I don't think it really matters who fault it is. What matters is that the kids learn to read before starting first grade, over the summer. All they would need is someone to read to them everyday and teach them the five, easy reading steps in this book.

It's disheartening when schools promote kids to the next grade without knowing how to read. If *all* elementary school teachers would include an hour a day of doing nothing but reading in their classrooms, I believe, it could put an end to adult illiteracy in our country. This reading hour could be used reading classics like "The Adventures of Tom Sawyer", "The Tale of Two Cities" and many other classics like these. The students could take turns reading. This will give the teacher a chance to hear each student read, and correct him/her, if necessary. It will also give the teacher a chance to teach his/her students new vocabulary words. It also gives the teacher an opportunity to see who is or who isn't reading on grade level and help him/her. If the teacher detects a child that can't read or isn't reading on grade level, he/she can arrange for the student to work with a reading specialist or teacher assistant two to three times a week. If the school doesn't have a reading specialist on staff, maybe the school could hire some local college students who are interested in going into the education field to help these kids learn to read. If they can't find any local college students to hire, they can put an ad in the paper for retired teachers, professors, and professionals to help these kids learn to read. In addition, this would be a great way to create some new jobs in America. Maybe "this idea" could even stimulate the economy. Now, if the school can't afford to hire someone, they can solicit volunteers to help. Reading the classics is a great way to help students learn new and challenging words, as well. "The Adventures of Tom Sawyer" is filled with adventure and lots of history of how things used to be. A small effort like this from schools everywhere could be the beginning to ending adult illiteracy in our country. It is important to teach our kids how to read as early as we can, so that they will not become discouraged and embarrassed in higher grades if they find themselves being the only one in the class that can't read.

Schoolchildren who do not know how to read or do basic math, will become further behind if someone doesn't intervene. This is another reason to work with your child at home and go over his/her homework (especially in elementary and junior high school); just in case your child's teacher doesn't notice, he/she needs some extra help.

A child who isn't reading by the second or third grade or on grade level is just the kind of thing that can be caught early, if we pay more attention to our kids. If caught ahead of time, teachers or parents can take the techniques and suggestions in this book and teach this child how to read.

Again, it's so important to teach our kids how to read and do arithmetic early, because it can avoid academic problems later. Teaching your child things early can potentially save your child from the embarrassment of not knowing how to do them later.

Give your child the kind of head start that every teacher would notice. Make sure you teach your child reading, math, and other skills during the summers, so that he/she can excel in the fall. Then, keep him/her ahead by working with him/her during the school year or enrolling him/her in a learning facility, like Kumon™. Remember, to encourage your child to read in their spare time to, because the more he/she reads, the more he'll/she'll know, and the more he/she knows, the farther he'll/she'll go.

I believe all schools should be required to put extra emphasis on reading comprehension, because it's just as important to know how to interpret what we read, as it is to know how to read. Most high school kids are required to take Biology, English, History, Algebra, and a Foreign Language class. Nonetheless, I feel they should also be required to take a "reading" class. In my opinion, there just isn't enough attention on developing reading comprehension and vocabulary. The ideal reading class in my opinion would focus entirely on reading, reading comprehension, vocabulary, and the root of all languages, "Latin". This Reading class would consist of students taking turns reading novels together, while the teacher listens and offers input. The students would also be required to write a one-page summary of each novel read in class. I think a class like this would help students perform better on standardized tests and do better in college. I also believe a class like this, if started in kindergarten, would help our kids become smarter and score higher on standardized and college admission tests. Nevertheless, we can do this at home with our own kids.

However, this isn't what is happening in most of our schools, because if everything was going right, we wouldn't have any illiterate adults in our country, now would we? Therefore, we have to make it our priority to teach and work with our own kids at home. We must see to it that our kids are reading on their grade levels, and that they understand what they are reading. Another thing we can do is to introduce our kids to websites like edhelper.com and clicknkids.com. These sites can help kids hone their reading skills and more. Edhelper.com has a category called Reading and Writing, where you can click on a sub-category called Reading Comprehension. This section will direct you to a page where you can choose your child's grade level and a reading selection from any of the following topics: Mysteries, Biographies, Animals, Science, and Poetry. You'll love edhelper.com because it also have other sections called Phonics, Kindergarten, Reading Skills, and more-- which can all be used to help your child practice his/her reading skills.

Most teachers are obviously capable of teaching our kids what is required at each grade level, yet we can't expect them to entirely notice or inform us if our children are not performing well in a particular subject (They can't just focus on your kids.). In today's world, we can't expect our doctors and nurses to tell us if something is wrong, and that's after receiving a good bill of health, just two weeks ago. In the same way, that is why we have to *be proactive* with our own health, as well as our kids' education. We must work with our kids at home, to give them a foundation that teachers can build on.

I really hope this book encourages every mother and father to teach their kids, while they are impressionable. This is truly the best head start we can give our kids. We must do this for our children if we want them to have a real chance at accomplishing their goals in the future. That is why I wrote this book, to encourage and convince parents like you to teach their children how to read, do arithmetic, and to teach them other skills early before they start kindergarten.

If you are reading this book, that means you care about making a difference in your child's life or some other child's life. Maybe it's your own child, your niece or nephew, or a child down at the local Boys and Girls Club you want to mentor and help reach his/her full potential. It doesn't matter really. What does matter is that you want them to learn and that you care. I applaud you, and I thank you. I'm glad you are concerned about giving our kids a real head start in school. Now, that we know it begins with us, let's do our part and motivate our kids to do their very best in school everyday.

You have a lot of work ahead of you, so why not get started now. Pick up a book today and read it to your child or volunteer as a parent reader in your child's classroom. Don't forget to play classical music at naptime or during homework time to keep those brain waves stimulated.

The next several pages contain actual reports and documentation that prove the methods in this book work. If you have been looking for some new ideas to make a change in your child's education, you've picked up the right book. Just check out my kids' reports on the following pages and be inspired to teach and tutor your child at home, too!

Spring-Ford Intermediate School
Award

SF

This certificate is presented to

Chelsea Davis

in recognition of participation in

and contribution to

The 6th Grade Honor Roll

2006 - 2007

William C. Marion
Principal

Dr. Dennis A. Booker
Activity Director

Spring-Ford Intermediate School
Award

SF

This certificate is presented to

Chelsea Davis

in recognition of participation in
and contribution to

The 5th Grade Honor Roll

2005-2006

William C. Marion
Principal

Activity Director

GIVE OUR KIDS A REAL HEAD START

Spring-Ford Area School District Intermediate/Middle School
7th Grade Center

833 South Lewis Road   Bldg. #2
Royersford, PA 19468

Telephone: 610-705-6010
Fax 610-705-8230

Homeroom: E208

June 16, 2008

Ms. Chelsea Davis
350 Vista Dr
Phoenixville, PA 19460

Dear Ms. Davis:

The purpose of this letter is to congratulate you for attaining Honor Roll. Achieving this status requires positive work ethic, dedication to studies, and commitment to excellence.

Congratulations on your academic successes in the classroom, outstanding educational growth, intellectual development in academics, and high motivation. The school district applauds you in your academic endeavors and encourages your continued educational development.

Sincerely,

Theresa M. Weidenbaugh

Theresa M Weidenbaugh
Principal

125

SPRING-FORD AREA SCHOOL DISTRICT
OAKS ELEMENTARY SCHOOL
P. O. Box 396
Oaks School Drive
Oaks, PA 19456
610-705-6008

Mark D. Moyer
Principal

Dear Parent/Guardian:

The Oaks Grade Level team has completed the end of the year literacy benchmark testing that is required by the *Response to Intervention* process. This assessment is designed to identify whether your child has reached grade level benchmarks or whether your child continues to work towards grade level benchmarks.

The results of the benchmark testing indicate that your child has met grade level benchmarks. Please continue to read with your child over the summer and encourage literacy activities.

If you have any questions about this assessment, kindly contact me. Thank you for your continued interest in your child's school success.

Sincerely,

Mark D. Moyer
Principal

GIVE OUR KIDS A REAL HEAD START

From: Carruthers, Rita <Rita.Carruthers@BellSouth.com>
To: 'Samantha.Davis@mindspring.com' <Samantha.Davis@mindspring.com>
Date: Friday, June 16, 2000 11:33 AM
Subject: THANK YOU

Samantha:

First of all, let us begin by saying THANK YOU! Thank you for your genuine love for children...Thank you for you kindness...Thank you for your patience...Thank you for your diligence...Thank you for your friendship. We could never express just how thankful we really are for all you have done for Aerial. She began attending Smart Tots right after her 3rd birthday, and it is amazing how much she has learned over the past two years. To our amazement, she began recognizing colors, reciting the alphabets, and counting after attending Smart Tots for only two weeks! It doesn't stop there...now she can recite those things in Spanish, recognize states on a US map(and continents on a world map), and read beginner books. You are truly wonderful!!!!

Not only do you enforce educational values, but you stress Christian values as well. HALLELUJAH!! It makes us so proud to listen to Aerial sing gospel songs, recite Bible verses, and even tell Bible stories that she learns in class. Out of all the schools we could have sent her to, we end up choosing one where the teacher is saved! GOD IS GOOD!!

The time is near for Aerial to leave Smart Tots and begin kindergarten. Due to the solid foundation you have provided, we are confident that she is more than ready. When you made the decision to teach, you made the right one. We truly believe you are doing what God wants you to do. You have been a blessing to us, and our prayers are with you constantly.

Sincerely,

Rita Carruthers

Individual Student Report

Student: DAVIS, CHELSEA A
GTID: 4146765217   Grade: 09
Class: MUSTAFAAC RACEEB
School: JOHNS CREEK
System: FULTON COUNTY SCHOOLS
Code: 868-0916
Test Date: SPRING 2010

Ninth Grade Literature & Composition

Report for :

DAVIS, CHELSEA A.

State Target Performance

Scale Score Range/Performance Levels

| | | 200 | DOES NOT MEET | 400 MEETS | 456 | EXCEEDS | 600 |

Scale Score	459
Performance Level	EXCEEDS
Grade Conversion	91

Scale Score: Number ranging from 200 to 600 which describes performance on this test.
Grade Conversion: Student's score converted to a 0-100 scale; score counts as 15% of course grade.

Performance Level Description:

The student's performance in Ninth Grade Literature & Composition EXCEEDS the standards set.

Students performing at this level demonstrate a comprehensive understanding of the structural elements and critical evaluation of various written materials. Students also show advanced knowledge of strategies used to enhance understanding across subject areas, including content and contextual vocabulary. Students are able to show in-depth knowledge of grade-level research techniques and display a strong ability to interpret the messages and effects of mass media. Students exceeding expectations display advanced knowledge of the writing process, including the usage and mechanics of Standard American English.

Domain Descriptions	Items Possible	Items Correct
Reading and Literature	23	19
Reading, Listening, Speaking & Viewing Across the Curriculum	17	14
Writing	14	13
Conventions	14	13

051710 8351 R00 080910-000000

Spring-Ford Area School District
Kindergarten Progress Report
School Year: 2007-2008

Student Name:Joshua Davis
School: **Oaks Elementary School**
Teacher: Miss Bortz

Indicators for Learner Qualities

1 = Consistently Demonstrates   2 = Developing   3 = Needs Improvement

QUALITIES OF A LEARNER	2nd	4th
Self-Directed Learner		
Works independently	1	1
Actively listens	1	1
Participates in class discussions	1	1
Stays on task	2	1
Demonstrates responsibility for self and belongings	2	1
Quality Producer		
Follows directions	2	1
Completes assigned tasks in allotted time	1	1
Produces work that is neat and organized	1	1
Produces legible handwriting	1	1
Demonstrates age-appropriate fine motor skills	1	1
Demonstrates age-appropriate eye-hand coordination	1	1
Collaborative Worker		
Works cooperatively with others	1	1
Respectful Citizen		
Demonstrates a positive attitude	1	1
Is courteous and considerate	1	1
Demonstrates respect for adults, peers, and property	1	1
Follows procedures and routines	2	1
Demonstrates self-control	2	2

Indicators for Academic Standards

P = Proficient — indicates that a student has demonstrated mastery on a given standard and is meeting or exceeding grade-level expectations

W = Working toward Proficiency — indicates that a student needs continued work or support on a given standard to meet proficiency

I = Improvement - indicates that a student is continuing to work toward proficiency and has made improvement since the last progress report (applicable in 4th marking period only)

Reading, Writing, Speaking and Listening	2nd	4th
1.1 Learning to Read Independently		
Identifies uppercase letters	26/26	26/26
Identifies lowercase letters	26/26	26/26
Produces consonant sounds	21/21	21/21
Produces short vowel sounds	5/5	5/5
Matches letters and sounds	P	P
Identifies rhymes	P	P
Segments and blends sounds	P	P
Reads high-frequency words	P	P
1.2 Reading Critically in All Content Areas		
1.3 Reading Analyzing and Interpreting		
Shows understanding of text and stories	P	P
1.4 Types of Writing		
Draws and/or writes to express ideas	P	P
1.5 Quality of Writing		
Uses phonics skills when composing words	P	P
Prints first name	P	P
Prints last name	P	P
Prints letters from memory	P	P
1.6 Speaking and Listening		
Listens responsively to stories and conversations	P	P
Presents information in front of a group	P	P
1.8 Research		
Locates information using appropriate sources and strategies	P	P

Mathematics	2nd	4th
2.1 Numbers, Number Systems, and Relationships		
Counts by 1s to 100	100/100	100/100
Counts by 10s to 100	100/100	100/100
Demonstrates one-to-one correspondence up to 20	P	P
Reads numerals 0-20	P	P
Writes numerals 0-20	P	P
Identifies coins by name	P	P
Identifies coins by value	P	P
2.2 Computation and Estimation		
Adds sets of objects	P	P
Subtracts sets of objects	W	P
2.3 Measurement and Estimation		
2.4 Mathematical Reasoning and Connections		
Determines instruments used for measuring	W	P
2.5 Mathematical Problem Solving and Communications		
2.6 Statistics and Data Analysis		
2.7 Probability and Predictions		
Records data on graphs	P	P
Analyzes graphs	W	P
2.8 Algebra and Functions		
Identifies, describes, and extends patterns	P	P
Sorts objects using various attributes	P	P
2.9 Geometry		
2.10 Trigonometry		
Identifies geometric shapes	P	P
2.11 Calculus		
Orders numbers 0-20	P	P

Science	2nd	4th
Understands and applies key concepts	P	P

Social Studies	2nd	4th
Understands and applies key concepts	P	P

Indicators for Special Subject Areas

1 Consistently Demonstrates
2 Developing
3 Needs Improvement

Physical Education	2nd	4th
Demonstrates progress in movement related skills	2	1
Demonstrates progress in manipulative skills		1
Demonstrates an understanding of physical education terminology and concepts	2	1

Art	2nd	4th
Follows basic art lesson expectations and safety procedures	2	1
Demonstrates an understanding of art terminology and concepts	2	1
Demonstrates progress in fine motor skills	2	1

Special Subject Area Comments

Teacher Comments

2nd Marking Period:
I am proud of Joshua's accomplishments and continue to enjoy watching him grow socially and academically. I enjoy Joshua's positive attitude, eagerness to learn, and wonderful ideas! It is a pleasure to him in my classroom.

4th Marking Period:
Thank you for being a part of our class Joshua! Keep practicing your skills over the summer! Thank you for always having a positive attitude! It will take you far! I hope you have a wonderful summer and best wishes next year in first grade!

Attendance	2nd	4th
Tardy	0	2
Absent	0	0

Your child has been assigned to First Grade for the upcoming school year.

131

Student	JOSHUA A. DAVIS	Grade	2
Birth date	2/17/2002	Class	COX
Gender	MALE	School	STATE BRIDGE
GTID	4031839103	System	FULTON COUNTY

Individual Student Report
Spring 2010

English/Language Arts   GPS

Level 3
Exceeds Standard
                                    910

◄ 900

Level 2
Meets Standard

◄ 800

Level 1
Does Not
Meet Standard

This student's score is **910**, which is in performance Level 3 and **exceeds the standard** for English/Language Arts.

A scale score of **910** indicates this student's achievement on the day of testing. If this student were to take the same test again, it is likely that his or her English/Language Arts score could be within the standard error of measurement range of 890 to 910.

English/Language Arts Domains

	Number Correct	Number Possible
Grammar/Phonics	30	30
Sentence Construction	12	12
Research	8	8

Performance Level 3 for English/Language Arts
The student's overall performance in ELA **exceeds the expectation** for this grade. Students who exceed the expectation have a clear understanding of English grammar. They easily use complete, complex sentences with correct subject/verb agreement and transitions. They consistently use question marks, commas in dates and letters, and periods after abbreviations. Students at this level successfully use appropriate resources to support word choices and share information (dictionary, thesaurus, and encyclopedia). Students who exceed the expectation show consistency in their writing, use of grammar, and research.

Mathematics   GPS

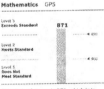

Level 3
Exceeds Standard   **871**

◄ 850

Level 2
Meets Standard

◄ 800

Level 1
Does Not
Meet Standard

This student's score is **871**, which is in performance Level 3 and **exceeds the standard** for Mathematics.

A scale score of **871** indicates this student's achievement on the day of testing. If this student were to take the same test again, it is likely that his or her Mathematics score could be within the standard error of measurement range of 857 to 885.

Mathematics Domains

	Number Correct	Number Possible
Number and Operations	33	33
Measurement	8	9
Geometry	10	12
Data Analysis and Probability	6	6

Performance Level 3 for Mathematics
The student's overall performance in mathematics **exceeds the expectation** for this grade. Students who exceed the expectation show a deep understanding of mathematical ideas and procedures. They solve various addition, subtraction, and multiplication problems with missing values. They understand fractions without visuals. They measure and describe and classify geometric figures and shapes. Students interpret and compare tables and graphs. They rarely make computation errors. They integrate multiple strategies to solve problems.

Go to the Georgia Department of Education website at **www.gadoe.org** for additional information about the CRCT and the Georgia Performance Standards.

Note:
Score Interpretation: A single score can provide only limited information. A student taking the same test three times might score higher or lower in each content area within a small range. Performance in the domain level should be interpreted with caution due to the limited number of items. Please regard decision information as an indication of a student's relative strengths and areas that may need improvement. Confirm this student's performance by reviewing classroom work, other standards-based assessments, and this student's progress reports during the year.

*Conditioned administration: A test score resulting from a conditioned administration must be interpreted in light of the specific accommodations provided the student during testing. Contact the teacher for specific accommodations provided this student.

CHAPTER X

Okay. I Get It.
So, Where Do I Begin?

As I've pointed out before, classic nursery rhymes are great stories to read to your younger children, especially when they are babies and toddlers. You may want to start with the ones you enjoyed as a child like: "Mary Had A Little Lamb", "Little Boy Blue", "Jack Be Nimble", and "Jack and Jill". For the older children, I would suggest starting with Dr. Seuss and The Little Golden books. You can even start a book collection for your child. It will be like your child's own personal library of Dr. Seuss and Little Golden books. Feel free to add other books your child likes. Keep in mind, these books will probably be your grandchildren's books one day, so don't forget to personalize them. For an example, try personalizing each book in your child's personal library with a special message like this:

To: Our Dearest Daughter Chelsea
Happy Birthday, Sweetheart~
May you enjoy this book for years to come!

133

From: Mom and Dad with all our love
Occasion: 1st Birthday

Again, just follow the steps and suggestions in this book, and I promise you that your child will learn how to read and get a *real* head start in school. What do I mean when I say "real" head start? Well, in the past head start programs were created to prepare kids for school, both socially and cognitively. Nevertheless, in my opinion, these programs just provided a free and safe haven for some toddlers, and if any learning occurred, I imagine it was very little. Consequently, we must teach our own kids how to read before they start school, along with some other things like writing, addition, subtraction, drawing, coloring, vocabulary, and spelling. This is my idea of a "real" head start. Then all you would have to do is continue working with your kids during the school year and over the summer to prepare them for the next grade. This is just the kind of dedication and effort it is going to take to make sure our kids graduate from high school on time.

Make it your mission to teach your child how to read and to master skills that will put him/her ahead of the curve. The more your child knows, the better prepared he'll/she'll be for school. You should also encourage and inspire your child to do his/her best as often as you can, and whatever you do, always believe in your child. Keep in mind, every child learns at his or her own pace and in different ways. That is why I have suggested several ways to teach your child how to read, and various tips and strategies to make your child smarter.

Read to your child everyday and choose books that will introduce him/her to new things. It's a smart thing to do during your child's daily reading time. If your child is following along and listening to you while you read, that's a good sign that he/she is paying attention. As your child grows, he'll/she'll probably start predicting what's going to happen next in the story. That's a good sign, that you're reading the story in an interesting way. Your child will use these reading skills in school one day, so continue teaching your child different things that will give him/her a jumpstart in school.

Keep in mind, some of you will find teaching your child how to read easy to do, but some of you may find that it's a longer process than you originally thought it was going to be. Don't give up! Just keep following the tips in this book, and I assure you that your child is going to learn how to read eventually. If your child learns how to *read well*, he'll/she'll more than likely *do well* in school, too. In addition, teaching your child how to read early can give your child an edge in school. Therefore, take some time to ask your child questions after you have read to him/her. This is a great way to test if your child is listening and paying attention to you. This is also a perfect time to introduce your child to reading comprehension. To help your child comprehend what you're reading to him/her or what he/she reads, just ask questions like: "Who are the characters in the story?", "Where is the story being taken place?", "What season is it?", and "What is going on in the story?" It will teach your child to listen carefully when he/she is read to or to pay attention when he/she is reading on his/her own. Enjoy the journey of teaching your child how to read and to *comprehend* what he/she is reading. Stay in the moment. Don't force or rush this reading experience, just let it come naturally, and it will.

Around the age of two-and-a-half or three years old, your child should be able to point out easy sight words to you like: *a, I, am, dog, cat,* and so on when you are reading to him/her. Again, this will only happen if you point to words while you are reading to your child, as you introduce and teach him/her the reading steps in this book. Don't forget to take advantage of the free reading activities offered at your local library, as well. It's a good idea to call ahead to get a schedule of events for toddlers and other age groups at the library. Your local library has tons of books your child can learn from, so stop by at least once or twice a week, okay?

I hope I'm encouraging you to be more involved in your child's education, because it's imperative that you do. It is important that you make sure your child retains what he/she is learning at school each day, too, by reviewing with him/her at home. You should always remind your kids to make good grades in school, and to listen and pay attention in class. Kids, who listen and pay attention in class, usually don't have to work so hard making good grades. Don't forget to hang up your child's accomplishments in school on the refrigerator or in his/her room to let him/her know how proud you are of him/her. We have to do whatever it takes to motivate America's kids to do well in school again. Encouraging kids everywhere to read is one way to keep them smart. Furthermore, I've found telling a child that he/she looks like a future lawyer or some other professional can really inspire him/her to do better in school. Therefore, going forward believe in your kids and remind them that they can become anything they want to become. Always stress the importance of getting a good education, because we all know that a quality education *is the ticket* that will help your child's dreams come true.

Progress reports should be viewed and taken seriously. It is always a smart idea to know where your kids stand in school. Good grades should naturally follow if your kids are attending school everyday on time, doing their homework, studying for all tests and quizzes, and listening in class. We must make our kids accountable for their own grades and actions in school. In other words, if your kids are doing well in school reward them for their efforts, but if they aren't, you must help them do better. One of the ways you can help your kids do better in school, is to make sure they do all of their homework, and that they study for every test and quiz. You should also check their grades online or ask the teacher to email you their current grades, when your kids want to go to a party, to the mall, or to the movies with their friends. Remember, kids respect, what you inspect. It's a tough thing to do, but if you are *consistent* in checking your kids' grades *every time they want to* go somewhere. I'm confident that your kids will do better in school. Now, this will only work if your rule is that your kids must have at least an 80 or above in all of their classes, with good comments in order to be allowed to go anywhere. In addition, don't forget to read to and with your kids a little everyday or on most days to keep them well informed. You must persuade your kids to do their best in school everyday, so that they'll be prepared to compete in tomorrow's world--which will obviously be faster and more advanced. Consequently, we must expect more from our children. After all, our kids are America's future.

Therefore, we have to do more than just *tell* our kids to do well in school; we have to help them make good grades in school. Although, competition isn't something we like to discuss with our children, we must, because it's the way of the land. Competition, whether we like it or not, is more prevalent than ever. Our children are competing whether they know it or not for the next spot in college, on a job, in the armed forces, on a sports team, in the music industry, in a performing arts school, and so on. We cannot deceive our kids about how the world works. We have to remind them to do their best in everything, so that their dreams will come true. It doesn't matter what our kids want to become, they'll be competing against other children with similar dreams.

We have to let them know, that in most cases, the most qualified gets the job. Think about it for a moment. Most of us have to compete everyday on our jobs and sometimes even during the Christmas season for that last toy on the shelf. Therefore, this is why we must teach our kids to do their best in school and in everything, so that they'll become educated and qualified enough to compete proficiently.

Nowadays, it isn't just good enough to "get the job", we all know that to "keep the job", we must stay current and competitive. Sometimes as adults, we find ourselves acquiring new skills just to keep up with today's demands. That is why it's a good idea to keep motivating your kids to learn as much as they possibly can, wherever they are. As I've stated before, the more our kids know, the more they grow, and the more they grow, the further they'll go.

We "must" help our kids obtain a quality education. Just as we encourage them to excel at sports, music, dance, and in other extra-curricular activities, we must also motivate them to do well in school. If we help and persuade our kids to do their best now, maybe they'll earn that scholarship to attend their favorite college later. There's no way around hard work. Our kids are going to have to be diligent about excelling in school, if they are serious about accomplishing their goals.

Who knows what could happen if you help your child reach his/her full potential? Your child may become the next Aretha Franklin, Arthur Ashe, Hillary Clinton or Dr. Phil. No one knows for sure, but we'll never know if we don't encourage our kids to dream BIG and to do their best at everything.

Work with your child at home, and teach him/her new things that will put him above the crowd. Encourage your child to complete all of his/her homework, to read all the time, and to study for tests in advance. Encourage your child to learn other things like a new instrument, a new language, some new math skills, or perhaps a new sport. Don't forget to have your child work on all or at least most of the websites mentioned in this book, as well. Some of them are free, and some of them may have a small fee, but it's worth it. In addition, if you have a laptop and wireless internet your child can work on his skills almost anywhere, even on the beach!

It's a good idea to give your child extra problems to work on or review math concepts like: addition, subtraction, number lines, multiplication, division, measurements, and algebra, so that he/she will remember how to solve these math problems on standardized tests. You should also take your child to the library to read all kinds of books. Just keep encouraging, motivating, and reminding your child to do his best on quizzes, homework, tests, and class projects, and I promise you your child will do well in school.

Another thing you should do, is make sure your child does his/her homework in a quiet area or at the library each day. Your child may insist that he/she can do his/her homework with the television on and the iPod blaring in his/her ears, but trust me he/she can't. How do I know? Well, I've let my own children talk me into letting them do their homework in front of the television, *and trust me it doesn't work*. Besides, if you don't give in as I did, your child will be able to complete his/her homework correctly, neatly, and in a timely manner. As stated before, give your child some free time after he/she completes all of his/her homework, before giving him/her any extra work you may want to give him/her to do. Mixing learning with a little fun goes a long way (as mentioned before), and it's a great way *not* to burn your child out or discourage him/her from learning. Don't feel bad about making sure your child does all of his/her homework or for giving him/her extra schoolwork to do at home to keep him/her ahead. It won't do him/her in, and it can only make him/her smarter. We all have heard the phrase before, "What doesn't take you out, can only make you stronger,"-- well that's exactly my point.

I hope your child is thinking about attending college after high school, because I believe it is going to take a little more than a high school diploma for your child to achieve his/her goals these days. Besides, college is the ideal place for kids to grow up (all the way) and stretch their minds a little more. You see, in college students have no other choice but to grow up and take responsibility for their own grades and actions.

Once you've seen to it that your child gets into college, hopefully on an academic, music or sports scholarship, remind him/her not to apply for a credit card on campus. Some companies will use your child's credit score after he/she graduates from college (good or bad) as a deciding factor to hire him/her or not (Unbelievable, right? I know, but so true!) For instance, if your child's credit score out of college is average, he/she may or may not get the job. I think using credit scores as a deciding factor to hire someone is unfair. In my opinion, a credit score (good or bad) can't tell you how someone would be like, as an employee. Nevertheless, realize that a potential employer doesn't know your child as you do. Unfortunately, it looks like credit scores are going to be around for a while, therefore, educate your child about credit, and help him/her build a credit score that will not only help him/her land the career of his/her dreams after college, but will also help him/her apply for a house or car. You may be thinking, "Isn't it a little early to be thinking about my child's credit score?"; Well, this is what this book is all about, giving your child a "real" head start in everything.

It's a good idea to start helping your child build a great credit score right before college or while in college, too.

One way you can do this, is by giving him/her a credit card, where you're the primary cardholder. This way you can keep track of your child's purchases, while helping him/her build his/her credit, and he'll/she'll be motivated to spend more wisely, knowing that you are going to get the bill at the end of the month.

Another thing, make sure your child obtains some work experience in his/her chosen field of study, because I remember the first question potential employers asked me after I graduated from college and it was, "What kind of work experience do you have for the job you're applying for?". Therefore, a college degree, decent credit, some work experience, and lots of prayer-- can go a long way.

That is why we must give our kids a "real" head start in everything. A "real" head start will help them shine in school and in extra-curricular activities. We must work with our children at home, so that they can do well in school. If kids are successful at school, they more than likely will go on to accomplish other goals. Please don't leave your child's future entirely in his/her hands. Our kids need us to see the big picture for them, because some of them can't see the forest for the trees. Besides, some kids need more guidance and re-directing than some, and that's okay, too. The best thing in the world is to "know your kids", and to encourage them where they are. Your child should never have to repeat ninth, tenth, eleventh, or twelfth grade. Just keep working with your kids at home and encouraging them to do their best in school, and I'm confident you'll see better grades and comments on your child's report card. Don't forget to reward your kids for doing a great job in school, because when they are older they will be compensated for doing a great job in their careers, too. Life is interesting, because you never have to explain success (it speaks for itself), but you'll always have to explain failure, as mentioned before.

So, help your child plan for his/her future, so he'll/she'll work diligently trying to make it happen.

These days it's easy to share bad news, because everyone all of a sudden is so interested in what you have to say. It's sad, but true! I mean we live in a world, where we want to see how "others" live, the good, bad, and the ugly. Just like the news, if it was "all good", nobody would want to watch. This is heartbreaking, but also true. Nevertheless, we have to remember to share "good news" about our kids to our family, friends, and neighbors. If your child hears you sharing wonderful things about him/her, it may inspire him/her to do more. Remember, focus on what your child is doing right not wrong, and assist him/her in those areas where he/she may need a little extra help. I cannot stress enough how powerful your compliments are! So, say complimentary things about your child always, to him/her and to others. After all, you are your child's first teacher and cheerleader. Saying the following phrases to your kids can go a long way: "Super job!" "I knew you could do it!" "Keep it up!" "Way to go!" "I love you!" "You're really great at this!" "You're an excellent reader!" "You'll get it next time!" and so on. Just remember to use words that will build your child up.

Remember, your child can become anything he/she wants to become, if he/she puts his/her mind to it. However, some kids have to be encouraged repeatedly to do their best in school; however, you should never get tired of helping and supporting your child to do his/her best. Our Heavenly Father is patient with us, so shouldn't we be patient with our kids, too? Some kids are what I like to call textbook kids. They go to school everyday and listen. They get along with all of their classmates. They do all their homework each day, and without being reminded to do it. They participate in class and do well on tests and quizzes (every teacher's dream).

On the other hand, some kids are every teacher's nightmare and every parent's, too (not exactly, but close-- nevertheless, we love them). These kids have to be constantly reminded to pay attention in class, respect their teachers and classmates, and to do their schoolwork. Whether or not we have the textbook kid or the allegedly nightmare kid (None of my readers' kids are nightmares, I'm sure.), it's important to remind all kids to respect their teachers, listen in class, do their schoolwork, study for their tests and quizzes, and to do their reports and projects on time. Remind them often why it is important to do well in school and reiterate that they are ultimately responsible for how they do in school. One of my favorite questions to ask schoolchildren is, "What would you like to be when you grow up?" My kids have no problem telling me what they would like to be when they grow up. Consequently, it gives me a chance to remind them to do their best in school, treat others the way they would like to be treated, to use their manners, to participate in extra-curricular activities after school, to work hard in sports and to do their best in everything they do, so that their dreams will come true. I also remind them that they are on their own after high school (not really--but I have to tell them something to get the results I'm looking for) unless they go to college. This way (hopefully) they'll work hard and smart in school, so that they will be accepted into a four year college. So, mom and dad, we must encourage our kids to do well, so that their American dream of receiving a quality education and living prosperous one day (so that they'll be a blessing to their family and to others), will come true.

We can and we should encourage our kids to do their best just as President Barack and Michelle Obama's, Hillary Clinton's, Martin Luther King, Jr.'s, and Bill Gates' parents did. These parents' kids contributed positively to society (some still are), and our lives are better today because of their efforts. Who knows, maybe you are raising the next household name? These parents saw something special in their kids, and I know we see something special in our kids, too! So, let's support our kids in everything they do, whether in the classroom or outside the classroom. You never know what the future holds. Some parents are famous today, because they encouraged their kids to dream BIG and to own and become it. For an example, Basketball Star Shaquille O'Neal's mom obviously encouraged him to do his best in basketball, and now she's a well-known author. She's the author of "Walk like You Have Somewhere to Go: From Mental Welfare to Mental Wealth" by Lucille O' Neal. *(17. http://today.msnbc.msn.com/id/36126004/ns/today-today_books).*

Another thing, your child should always feel special and loved everyday, even if he/she isn't getting his/her way. There is a way to say no to your child or correct him/her in love, and it's called being consistent. What is being consistent? Well, when you are consistent, your child knows what you expect from him/her. If you aren't consistent, your child won't believe it when you say you're going to ground him/her for not following the rules, especially, if you are the kind of parent that gives in easily. Therefore, it is important to say what you mean and mean what you say, because your child will come to respect what you carry out. For an example, let's say the rule in your house is to bring home at least all A's and B's on your report card or lose your cell phone and Facebook™ privileges. Instead, your child brings home mostly C's, 1 B, 1A, and 1high D (almost a C, but not) on his/her report card, and the first thing you think to do is screech at him/her. Then, after you become cool, calm, and collected again, your child ask you can he/she go to the movies with a couple of his/her friends from school. Before you know it, you're dropping your child off and his/

her friends at the movies, and before you drive off, he/she yells, "I'll call you mom from the movies when it's over!" (Of course, he'll/she'll be calling you from his/her cell phone you said he/she wouldn't be allowed to use.). Wow! Guess what mom and dad, you weren't consistent. You didn't ground your child at all from the cell phone or from Facebook™ (this is where your child found out about meeting his/her friends at the movies), instead you let him/her go to the movies anyway. I must admit it's hard sometimes to be consistent, but we must, if we want our kids to reach their full potentials one day.

If we could motivate every child in America to go to school everyday and give a hundred percent, more of our kids would graduate from high school and on time. Somehow, we must persuade our kids how important an education is, and that a good education is usually the *key* to unlocking their future. We have to find a way to convince our kids that education is a valued commodity in our country and around the world; and that in order to obtain one, it is going to take a lot of diligence and perseverance on their part.

Our kids are going to make it, because you and I are the kind of parents who will see to it. We are the parents who do whatever is necessary to get results (within the law, of course). We correct, encourage, motivate, inspire, and pray for our children. We ask the right questions, and we give our kids the tools to succeed. I believe every parent that reads this book will be inspired to help their kids reach their goals. It is going to take the right attitude and a whole lot of work from our kids, for their dreams to come true. Yet, I believe in our kids and in our schools, and if everyone does his/her part, we won't need Superman anymore!

We must also emphasize to our children, the importance of dressing appropriately for school and other occasions. We live in a world where we are first judged by the way we look.

People will either respect or disregard you; therefore, we must encourage our kids to present their best selves in the world (because we are in the world, but we don't have to be of the world). I believe a child that looks his best, does his best. Subsequently, I think it is important how we send our kids dressed to school each day. It sends a nonverbal message to their teachers, peers and everyone else how to treat them. I am not suggesting you dress your child like he/she is going on an interview, but he/she should always look neat and well groomed from head to toe. It shouldn't surprise us that the world judges you by how you look, because the bible tells us, "The LORD does not look at the things man looks at. Man looks at the outward appearance, but the LORD looks at the heart." *(18. 1 Samuel 16:7 NIV)* Therefore, parents, it is up to us to encourage our kids to brush their teeth, tie their shoestrings, and groom their hair everyday. Besides, we want everyone to treat our kids with respect whether we are present or not, right? Well, let's send our kids to school dressed neatly, everyday, and remind our teenage boys to pull up their pants and our teenage girls to wear their camisoles.

When you decide to give your kids a real head start in school, you're signing up for 13 long years of motivating your child to act and do his/her best in school. My point is this. Saying it is easy, but actually doing it, well that's another story. Some days will be easy, and to be honest with you, some days will be down right challenging. Our kids will probably defy us sometimes, but we can't give up on them. You can't throw in the towel now, because you've invested too much time and energy teaching your child how to read and giving him/her a real head start in everything. We have what it takes to run the race with our children, if we have to. It is our job to correct, guide, and motivate our children all the way to the finish line. This is what we do. For the days, you want to pull out your hair, because despite your efforts your kids seem to be going in the opposite direction-- "Don't!" "I've been there, and trust me, it gets easier." Our kids aren't perfect and neither are we (if we're honest). Sometimes, you'll find yourself constantly persuading your child to do his/her best in school and in extra-curricular activities.

Well, we have no other choice but to encourage our kids to do their best now, because right now they aren't thinking about how they are going to support themselves in the future. Right now, they are more concerned about their *social lives*, than they are about their *future lives*. Our kids need us to prepare them for when they grow up. Most of them want to become rock stars, super athletes, movie stars, reality stars, talk show hosts, models, doctors, lawyers, CPAs, and dentists anyway. I think it's fantastic for our kids to dream BIG and an extraordinary way, because they might just become any of these. So do encourage your kids to go after their dreams with all of their might and grit. Nevertheless, remind them of these professions, because someone has to do them (and some of them make a lot of money, too) like entrepreneurs, authors, news reporters, teachers, nurses, bank tellers, chefs, nurses, designers, business professionals, grocery store managers, computer specialists, and hotel managers. Nonetheless, we should encourage our kids that nothing is out of their reach, but we must also let them know of all the possible careers they can do for a living someday, too. We must tell our kids that knowing how to read, write, and do math is necessary, regardless of what they decide to go into. Therefore, making sure your kids receive a quality education is a smart thing to do, regardless of what they decide to grow up and become.

Martin Luther King, Jr., was an inspiration to kids and adults alike everywhere. One day he asked a group of kids an important question, and the following is what Dr. King had to say to them. I think it will inspire you to encourage your kids to stay in school and do their best.

""I want to ask you a question, and that is: What is your life's blueprint?

Whenever a building is constructed, you usually have an architect who draws a blueprint, and that blueprint serves as the pattern, as the guide, and a building is not well erected without a good, solid blueprint.

Now each of you is in the process of building the structure of your lives, and the question is whether you have a proper, a solid and a sound blueprint.

I want to suggest some of the things that should begin your life's blueprint. Number one in your life's blueprint should be a deep belief in your own dignity, your worth and your own self. Don't allow anybody to make you feel that you're nobody. Always feel that you count. Always feel that you have worth, and always feel that your life has ultimate significance.

Secondly, in your life's blueprint you must have the basic principle the determination to achieve excellence in your various fields of endeavor. You're going to be deciding as the days and as the years unfold what you will do in life — what your life's work will be. Set out to do it well.

And I say to you, my young friends, doors are opening to you--doors of opportunities that were not open to your mothers and your fathers — and the great challenge facing you is to be ready to face these doors as they open.

Ralph Waldo Emerson, the great essayist, said in a lecture in 1871, "If a man can write a better book or preach a better sermon or make a better mousetrap than his neighbor, even if he builds his house in the woods, the world will make a beaten path to his door."

This hasn't always been true — but it will become increasingly true, and so I would urge you to study hard, to burn the midnight oil; I would say to you, don't drop out of school. I understand all the sociological reasons, but I urge you that in spite of your economic plight, in spite of the situation that you're forced to live in — stay in school.

And when you discover what you will be in your life, set out to do it as if God Almighty called you at this particular moment in history to do it. Don't just set out to do a good job. Set out to do such a good job that the living, the dead or the unborn couldn't do it any better.

If it falls your lot to be a street sweeper, sweep streets like Michelangelo painted pictures, sweep streets like Beethoven composed music, sweep streets like Leontief Price sings before the Metropolitan Opera. Sweep streets like Shakespeare wrote poetry. Sweep streets so well that all the hosts of heaven and earth will have to pause and say: Here lived a great street sweeper who swept his job well. If you can't be a pine at the top of the hill, be a shrub in the valley. Be the best little shrub on the side of the hill.

Be a bush if you can't be a tree. If you can't be a highway, just be a trail. If you can't be a sun, be a star. For it isn't by size that you win or fail. Be the best of whatever you are.""

(19. From the estate of Dr. Martin Luther King, Jr. "What Is Your Life's Blueprint?: http://seattletimes. nwsource.com/special/mlk/king/words/blueprint. html *Six months before he was assassinated, King spoke to a group of students at Barratt Junior High School in Philadelphia on October 26, 1967.*

CHAPTER XI

Teaching Your Child
How To Read & Other Skills

In order to teach your child how to read, he/she must learn the alphabet first. You may be thinking my child already knows his/her ABCs. Well, I hope so, but if your child can *only* sing the alphabet song, he/she doesn't know his/her ABCs. Your child should be able to recognize and sound out each letter. He/She should also be able to tell you a vowel from a consonant. If he/she knows all of the above, then your child knows his/her ABCs, and he/she can skip reading steps one, two, and three. Well, for the rest of you, let's get busy! **Step 1, read to your child as often as you can and teach your child how to sing the alphabet song**. For the next month or so, you may feel like a Preschool or Kindergarten teacher, because you will spend a lot of time teaching your child how to sing the alphabet. Sing the alphabet song around your child, and he'll/she'll sing it along with you. Sing it at bath time, naptime, and bedtime to teach your child the alphabet song. Just keep it fun and your child will enjoy learning how to sing the alphabet song.

A good time to start introducing your child to the alphabet is right around thirteen months or older. To introduce your child to the alphabet go out and buy a children's CD with the traditional alphabet song on it. Next, play the CD often to teach your child how to sing the alphabet song. It's important that you sing along with your child, because it will help him/her learn it faster. It's a passive way to teach your child to sing the alphabet song. Play the CD in your car, at bath time, on long trips, at naptime, on play dates, or just for fun to help your child learn to sing the alphabet song. After awhile, your child will start to learn all of the songs on the CD, especially the alphabet song. When your daughter or son can sing the entire alphabet song by herself/himself, *clearly and completely*, he/she is ready for the second step in the reading process. **Step 2, teach your child the letters of the alphabet, all 26 letters, upper and lowercase letters.** A great way to teach your child the letters of the alphabet, is to go out and buy an ABC border for your child's room, and point to each letter, while you sing the alphabet song together. You can buy these letters at any teacher supply store. While you're there, pick up a teacher's pointer, and use it to point to all the letters as you and your child sing the alphabet song together. This will help your child learn to recognize his/her ABCs better. Remember, do this at least twice a day at different times, and your child will be able to name all 26 letters by himself/herself. It's important to teach your child how to identify both upper and lower case letters. Your child should be able to recognize all capital and lower case letters before moving on to step three. Go to www.mrsjonesroom.com for more fun ways to teach your child the alphabet.

Before we move on to step three, let me bring a few more things to your attention. It's important to relax and have fun while you are teaching your child the letters of the alphabet, because he/she will naturally pay more attention if you do. The idea here is to sing the alphabet song in an *upbeat tone*, while pointing to each letter. You should encourage your child to sing with you, while he/she is watching you point to each letter. Next, point to each letter without singing the alphabet song this time, and encourage your child to say each letter aloud. If he/she has a little trouble remembering any of the letters, don't hesitate to help him/her, and move on to the next letter.

Bear in mind, it's easier for a child to learn words if he/she knows the letters of the alphabet, and if he/she can read words he/she will eventually read sentences. That is why it's important that your child learn all 26 letters, both upper and lower case letters very well. It may take your child two weeks, months or even years to learn steps 1 and 2. It all depends on your child's age and readiness. Just remember to be patient, and your child will learn to sing and recognize the letters of the alphabet in his or her own time. Don't compare your child to others, while he/she is learning any of the five reading steps in this book, because teaching your child how to read is going to take a lot of patience on your part.

Therefore, make a decision to teach your child each reading step thoroughly, and I'm confident that he/she will learn to read. In addition, if you work with your child just a little everyday teaching him/her other basic skills, you'll be amazed at how much he/she learns in such a short time. I believe every child has the ability and the brain capacity to learn anything someone takes the time to teach him/her. Just encourage your child to *listen to you when you're teaching him/her different things, because a child that listens well... learns well*. It will also prepare him/her to listen in school one day when he's/she's old enough to go. You must give your child lots of love and encouragement, but you must also sit down and teach him/her different skills early to give him/her a head start in school. Just keep singing the alphabet song with your child, as you or your child point to each letter, and I'm confident he'll/she'll learn steps one and two. You can also play "fish" and "matching" with a set of alphabet cards. You can usually pick up a pack of alphabet cards at any teacher supply store or at Walgreens. These are fun games to teach your child the alphabet, and a great way for your child to practice his/her ABCs.

Remember to read to your child often, as you teach him/her each step, and review the alphabet flash cards with your child at least once or twice a day. When reviewing the alphabet cards with your child, ask him/her to tell you the letter on each card. Another great idea is to have your child put the cards in alphabet order, while singing the alphabet song. Don't forget to give your child lots of praise while he/she is learning the alphabet. If your child needs help singing the alphabet song or saying the letters, just help him/her.

Think about it. When you want to accomplish a goal, don't you do what it takes to get it done? Of course, you do. Everyone does. Well, this is exactly the kind of commitment I am asking you to make while you teach your child the five easy reading steps in this book. Just stay unswerving (steady, unchanging) and motivated and your child will learn how to read.

Now, that your child knows how to sing the alphabet song and can identify each letter, he's/she's ready for **Step 3, which is all about vowels and consonants**. The best way to introduce your child to vowels and consonants is to tell him/her that vowels and consonants can be found in every American word and name. In addition, tell him/her that vowels are "a", "e", "i", "o", "u", and sometimes "y" and that all the remaining letters are called consonants. Point out vowels and consonants in names and words by circling the vowels and underlining the consonants, to teach your child the difference between a vowel and a consonant. Next, have him/her do it with his/her first and last name and with other words, until he/she gets the idea. You may have to review this concept daily with your child until you're sure he/she knows how to recognize a vowel and a consonant. Now, that your child knows how to sing the alphabet song, can identify upper and lower case letters, and can tell you the difference between a vowel and consonant, he's/she's ready for step four, which is learning the sound of each letter. Don't forget to use Mrs. Jones' website to help your child practice the alphabet. Go to www.mrsjonesroom.com and scroll down to the alphabet activities link and double-click to enter the website. This wonderful website will help your child learn the letters of the alphabet and the sounds they make. Don't forget to bookmark this website under your favorite websites. Use this website daily to help your child learn the alphabet and lots of other things. There are many activities on this website to keep your child busy and motivated, as he/she learns the letters of the alphabet and how to read. Try working on one letter a day or several letters a day, whatever is comfortable for you and your child.

You should repeat any steps you think your child needs to review. I have found that early exposure and repetition are the keys to teaching your kids anything.

Here are three additional websites that can help your child practice the alphabet and learn to read: www.starfall.com, www.edhelper.com, and www.clicknkids.com (use samanthadavis@comcast.net for a discount on this website). There is a small fee to use some of these websites, but certainly worth the money. On www.edhelper.com, you'll find worksheets you can print that will help your child practice writing the letters of the alphabet and mini-books your child can make, color, and read on his/her own.

When your child learns to read, encourage him/her to read stories aloud. This way, you can help him/her pronounce any words he/she doesn't know very well. If you have the time, look up these words in the dictionary or just tell your child what they mean. The Biscuit Book Series are great books for new readers to read on their own. So, don't forget to add these books to your child's home library. These books can be purchased on www.amazon.com , at your local bookstore, or checked out at your local library.

If your child hasn't learned steps one, two, or three yet, continue teaching him/her these steps until he/she learns each step. Have your child practice the ABCs using his/her flashcards, while you're at the grocery store, running errands, or at the doctor's office. This is exactly the kind of dedication it is going to take for your child to learn every reading step in this book. If he/she learns them well, he/she will eventually learn to read well.

I also have included a hundred plus websites in this book that will help your kids get a real head start in kindergarten and stay ahead in grades K-12th grade. Make sure your kids visit these websites to learn vocabulary, science, and other things to supplement your child's education. Remember, standardized tests are impartial, in other words, your child doesn't get extra points because he/she attends a high-performing school or points taken away because he/she attends a low-performing school, *your child's test scores are calculated on what **he/she knows***. Therefore, make sure your child work on grade-appropriate websites (it's okay to work on a higher grade), so that your child will learn many things to give him/her, an edge in school and on standardized tests. In other words, teach your child at home in addition to what he/she is learning at school. I saw the movie, "Waiting For "Superman", nevertheless, I'm going to encourage you to work with what you got and don't wait for Superman, a school lottery, or a teacher to determine your child's fate or future. I don't care if your child attends a private, charter, boarding, or public school do not leave your child's education entirely in anyone's hand. No one cares like you do or sees your child's potential like you can. So, do your research, find out what other states and countries are learning at certain grade levels and find websites, books, and other resources that will teach your child what he/she should know. This will help him/her do well on tests like the PSAT, SAT, ACT, and other standardized tests. Then, after your child makes it into college one day, continue encouraging him/her to do his/her best, because he/she will need good grades to land his/her dream career or to go on to law or medical school. One of the best things we can do for our kids, is to encourage them to turn off the television, cell phones, and the computer when they are doing their homework or studying for a test or quiz. If your child is using the computer to work on some of the websites mentioned in the back of this book or to do research, that's understandable, but make sure your child is using the computer in front of you.

Teaching your child how to read is one of the most important things you can do to give your child a true head start in kindergarten. When a child learns to read, he/she can reason, understand, and learn almost anything. Remember, the kindergarten students who went to school a whole school year and didn't learn how to read? Well, this doesn't have to happen to your child. It wasn't anyone's fault either. Yet, this is just the sort of thing that can happen to our kids, if we leave our kids' education in someone else's hand. Therefore, continue teaching your child how to read and to do some other things to give him/her a *real* head start in school.

By now, your child probably knows how to sing the alphabet song. He more than likely can point to and say all of his ABCs, and he/she probably knows the difference between a vowel and a consonant. Now, concerning vowels and consonants, make sure your child can confidently tell you that a, e, i, o, u and sometimes y are vowels and that the rest of the letters are consonants before moving on to step four.

If your child has learned steps one, two, and three, and you feel like he/she is ready for step four, by all means proceed. On the other hand, if you feel he/she needs more time on one of the steps, that's perfectly okay, too, because he/she will learn them eventually. Just continue encouraging and reviewing steps two and three with your child, and don't forget to teach with lots of love and praise. After your child has mastered steps one, two, and three, he/she is ready to move on to step four. **Step 4, is a lot of fun, because you will be teaching your child the sounds of the alphabet and how to write them.** Don't forget to use www.edhelper.com and www.first-school.ws to print off worksheets to have your child practice writing the letters of the alphabet, as he/she learns the sounds of the alphabet. You can use crayons, markers, glitter, buttons, and strips of cloth to decorate and make letters, too! Just keep it fun and creative and your child will learn the sounds of the alphabet and how to write them soon, and so much more!

Remember, if you feel in your heart that your child needs a little more time on any of the four steps above, that's completely okay. Give your child the time to learn them comfortably. This is not a contest or a race. We have to give our kids room to grow and room to make mistakes. This is how they learn. Nevertheless, you may want to stop now and re-teach your child the steps you feel he/she needs to review before moving on to step four. Do not move on to step five until you are confident that he has mastered steps one through four.

Again, you shouldn't worry if your child isn't learning the steps fast enough, because we are not trying to teach your child anything quickly. We are trying to teach your child a skill he'll/she'll use for the rest of his/her life. So, just remember to be loving and patient while you're teaching your child these reading steps. Keep it fun and allow room for your child to make mistakes and he'll/she'll learn these steps effortlessly. Step five, will encourage you to introduce and teach your child 128 Super Words Every New Reader Should Know in Chapter 12.

You should read to your child often while you are teaching him/her the reading steps in this book. It gives your child an idea how to read and he/she learns a great deal, as well. As your child learns to read different words, encourage him/her to read titles of books, bulletin boards, cereal boxes, happy meal bags and street signs as you go throughout the day to help him/her practice reading different words. Keep following the tips and strategies in this book, and you'll begin to see a lot of progress in your child's reading.

Remember, when you make reading and learning a priority in your home, whether you're playing Trivia with your kids or reading a family devotion together after dinner, anything that involves reading will naturally make your kids more knowledgeable about many different things. Just keep reading and teaching your child how to read, and I'm, confident he'll/she'll get a "real" head start in school.

Don't give in to the idea that your child may be too young to learn how to read as I've mentioned before. I believe it's never too early to teach your child how to read or teach him/her anything that can give him/her a head start in school. Remember, your main goal is to give your child an extraordinary head start, not just an ordinary head start. That's why it's important to start teaching your child how to read early, because reading is the foundation of learning. Your child will not learn how to read over night, so please don't expect him/her to. Learning is a process, and it takes time, patience, love and lots of room for mistakes. So, take it slow and teach your child at least one thing a day that will help him/her learn to read and get a head start in school.

As mentioned before, teaching anyone how to read takes time and patience. That is why it is imperative that you start as early as you can. Start by reading and singing to your baby, as often as you can. Then, when he/she gets a little older, read to him/her while he/she sits in the stroller or stands in a walker. Sure, he/she may become distracted and may not even seem interested sometimes, but if he/she is old enough to watch "Barney or Sesame Street" on television, then he's/she's ready to listen to you read to him/her for five or ten minutes. Try it and see for yourself!

Remember, the earlier you start the better; because it may take several years before your child is ready to move on to step two. There will be days when you feel like saying, "This isn't as easy as I thought it was going to be." Well, anything worth accomplishing, never is. Never let someone convince you that it is too early to start teaching your child how to read. Actually, the earlier you begin teaching your child how to read or to do anything, the better off he/she will be.

Whatever you do, don't send your child to kindergarten not knowing how to read, because he/she may be left behind on the first day of school. Do you really want to take a chance sending your child to kindergarten thinking he'll/she'll learn to read before first grade? Really? Don't do it. Teach your child how to read before you enroll him/her in kindergarten. I really believe my kids are doing well in school today, because they learned to read early, along with some other things. So, teach your own child how to read before enrolling him/her in school.

Some parents believe that learning to read just rather happens one day in school. Well, maybe, but again, why take a chance? Teach your child how to read yourself. This way you'll know for sure that your child knows how to read in every grade. In addition, putting my tips into practice will help you teach your child not only how to read but inspire you to give him a head start in other things like: addition, science, subtraction, social studies, multiplication, geography, division, fractions, decimals, poetry, foreign language, vocabulary, basic algebra, and basic geometry. When teaching your child new things at home, using the websites mentioned in this book, remember to instruct him/her on his/her grade level. Here's a story that will *inspire* you to teach your child some things early. Well, just the other day, Joshua came home from school and shared with me that he helped some of his fellow classmates with their long division problems, after finishing his early. How cool was that? I taught him how to do long division in second grade! He also got a chance to practice them over the summer, before starting third grade. Try doing this with your child at home, too! Remember, reading and learning begins in the home.

Can you hear me cheering and clapping for you? Well, I'm applauding your efforts and dedication to give your child a real head start in school and in other areas!

Now, that you have successfully taught your child how to read and have officially given him/her a head start in kindergarten, celebrate by going to Barnes & Noble. While you're there, buy your child a new book and share a treat together in their cafe area. Now, all you have to do is keep your child ahead throughout the school year, by working with him/her at home.

I am sure that your child will succeed in school, if you keep putting the tips and strategies in this book into practice. Anything you can teach or introduce your child to at home, before his/her teacher teaches it to him/her can and will give your child an advantage in school. Consequently, you should always remind your child to do his/her best at everything, because it will increase his/her chances of accomplishing his/her goals someday.

I love reading and teaching my kids new things, because children, whether they say it or not, enjoy learning about new things. They also soak up knowledge, like a sponge soaks up water. I saw first hand, the positive effects of teaching my kids new things at home. Kids, who learn new things at home, as well as what they learn at school, naturally feel more confident. Therefore, keep reading, playing classical music, and teaching your child new things (especially new words on www.wordlywise.com) at home, and he/she will excel in school and on standardized tests. We all know that when you read, you learn--right? In contrast, we may not be so sure about how classical music helps us learn; nevertheless, I believe classical music is effective, and can make your child brighter. Why? Well, my kids and the kids I taught at my learning center seemed to pay more attention in class, when I played classical music for them. Consequently, play classical music for your kids, because the more your kids pay attention, the more they will learn, and the more they learn, the smarter they'll become.

Before I forget, when you read to your child, make sure he/she knows that you read from left to right. You may want to glide your index finger from left to right, to illustrate as you read. Don't forget to mention how following the rules of punctuation marks like periods, question marks, exclamation points, and commas make it easier for us all to read.

When your child begins reading words on his/her own, let him/her know how proud you are of him/her by giving him/her a BIG hug. When you take a moment to congratulate small successes like these while teaching your child different things along the way, can make a HUGE difference in your child's attitude towards school and about learning.

CHAPTER XII

128 Super Words
Every New Reader Should Know

In this chapter, you will find 128 super words to teach your child how to read, that in my opinion, every beginner reader should know. I believe the following words will help your child read with ease. Try putting them on flash cards and have your child practice them a little everyday, and he/she will learn them in record time. In addition, after putting the words on flash cards, you should tape a set up in your child's room to help him/her learn and retain them better. When you use various methods to teach your child new things, he/she learns information better.

The 128 words in this chapter will have your child whizzing through basic sentences in no time. Keep putting the suggestions and techniques in this book into practice, and your child will get a real head start in reading and in school. If your child has not mastered steps one through four, take some time to re-teach them to your child. On the other hand, if your child has mastered steps one through four, proceed to step five.

Step 5, read to and encourage your child to read with you, while you introduce and teach him/her the 128 super words below. It may take several weeks or months before your child learns them all, and that's totally okay. Just remember to be patient and unwavering, and your child will learn them.

I	can	bat	it	pig	his	how	so
am	fan	cat	bit	cow	the	all	up
a	man	fat	fit	dog	fed	did	ate
no	pan	hat	hit	mom	led	ate	did
yes	ran	mat	her	dad	bow	if	hen
at	van	rat	pit	he	sis	our	bin
as	we	pat	sit	she	nine	in	lay
in	see	sat	eat	who	us	is	bed
on	zoo	do	that	son	up	down	go
row	low	mouse	seven	our	win	jog	do
won	mow	house	den	and	bend	cup	to
had	bun	hot	an	set	send	bone	three
bad	fun	dot	eye	ant	ten	cone	four
sad	eight	cot	too	day	then	one	five
mad	run	got	wow	now	that	two	six
sun	way	jot	day	bug	us	bee	see

CHAPTER XIII

Never Give Up

By this stage in the book, your child should be reading if he/ she has mastered steps one, two, three, four, and five. If your child isn't reading yet, don't worry about it. Just re-introduce steps two through five (I'm assuming your child knows how to sing the alphabet clearly), and I'm confident he'll/she'll be reading soon. You must also take into account, your child will learn at his/her own pace. Your job is to help him/her get there! Keep reading to your child and encouraging his/ her efforts, and he/she will learn to read.

I know I've mentioned this before, but ask your child questions when you read to him/her or with him/her. It encourages him/her to pay more attention. Ask him questions like, "What do you think will happen next in the story?" or "Who are the main characters in the story?" He/ She may have answers for you, but then again, he/she may not. The most important thing is to encourage your child to listen and pay attention when he/she is read to or pay attention when he/she is reading on his/her own.

More importantly, don't give up on teaching your child

how to read, if he/she isn't reading yet, because you are ultimately teaching him/her a skill that he/she will use in kindergarten, elementary school, middle school, high school, college, and in his/her career someday. Reading to your child and teaching him/her how to read early, will give your child a head start in school and in life. When you raise a *reader*, you raise a *leader*.

Have you ever heard of Polite Stewart, Jr.? Well, he's a young man who started college at fourteen years old, isn't this incredible? I'm not suggesting that we make our kids smart enough to start college at fourteen years old, because in my opinion, you should be both socially mature, as well as academically prepared to handle college. The majority of us probably wouldn't want our children to leave for college at fourteen years old anyway-- right? In any case, I'm merely referencing Polite Stewart's story, because he was reading at three years old and was very diligent (at such an early age) when it came to learning. Our kids must also be self-motivated, because we can only teach and encourage them to do their best, we can't go to school for them. Let me get back to why I feel the need to reference Polite Stewart. In addition to reading early and armed with an industrious attitude, he also was enthusiastic and eager to be taught (God blesses the child who is born with a healthy dose of self-motivation). Stewart also began college one whole year before Martin Luther King, Jr. did! I was so impressed with Polite Stewart that I had to find out what inspired him. I wanted to know how his parents raised such a brilliant scholar. I hope his story motivates you to create an environment in your home that is conducive to learning. I know it made me look for new ways I could help educate my kids at home (…and I have included them in this book), and it gave me a new determination to help my kids succeed at everything. *45.*

http://www.2theadvocate.com/news/education/19520584. html *and Essence Magazine 2010*

Nevertheless, here's Polite Stewart Jr.'s story. He was home schooled and was reading, writing and doing arithmetic all at the age of three. Okay, there are no surprises here, because my kids were reading, writing, and doing arithmetic at the age of three, too. Don't forget the strategies in this book can help you teach your child how to read, write, and do arithmetic early, also. Anyhow, I kept reading his story, because I wanted to see was there *anything* about Stewart's life that I could share in this book that would help you assist your child in his/her studies. Guess what? I discovered that Stewart was an exceptionally, bright child who had a natural curiosity for learning. My line of reasoning is that he enjoyed learning and wanted to learn, like Abraham Lincoln did. I was a little disappointed, because I wanted to believe that his parents were the reason he was so smart. Then, it occurred to me that our kids, just like Stewart, must have a strong desire to learn, set goals for themselves, and then do what it takes to accomplish those goals. *46.* http://www.2theadvocate.com/news/education/19520584. html *and Essence Magazine 2010*

We can inspire, encourage, and motivate our kids to learn, but it will ultimately be up to them how much they learn and retain. We cannot follow our kids to school or college. We can only spoon-feed our kids for so long, because as the old saying goes, "You can give a man fish to eat for one day, but if you teach him how to fish, he'll eat for the rest of his life." Another saying goes like this, "You can lead a horse to water, but you can't make it drink." In other words, we can encourage our kids to do their best in school, but we can't make them learn. What we can do is provide our kids the necessary resources to succeed at learning in school. We can also give them our love, time, and energy to help them strive in school and in after school activities.

Therefore, working with your child over the summer can give him/her a boost in the upcoming school year, and continuing to work with him/her throughout the school year can keep him/her ahead. Although, your diligence in helping your child get smart and stay smart, can give him/her a jump start in school, at some point, your child must take charge of his/her own actions and efforts in school. How do you teach a child accountability? Well, I believe half of it comes from within, and the other half begins at home. We have to give our kids things to be responsible for at home, so that they can learn how to be responsible for themselves. For instance, when a child is responsible for a pet or a younger sibling, he/she realizes that the pet or his/her younger sibling is depending on him/her. It makes your child step up and he/she does what is expected of him/her. Therefore, let's keep encouraging our kids to do their best in school, so that they'll grow up and become what they want to be in the future. Think about it for a moment. Every child dreams of becoming something great, right? So, why shouldn't you help him/her achieve his/her goals? For that reason, use the summers to teach your child new skills and encourage him/her to read all summer long, because the more he/she knows, the further he'll/she'll go, as I've mentioned before.

So, continue working with your child at home, as well as sending him/her to school each day, and don't forget to make sure your child gets a good night's rest and a good breakfast before going to school. It doesn't matter if you home school your children or not, always give him/her some extra schoolwork to do, outside of school requirements.

In addition to teaching your child how to read, make sure you teach him/her some common sense things like: how to write his/her first and last name, learn his/her address, and be able to tell someone his/her parents' names before starting kindergarten. He/She should also know how to write a letter and do arithmetic. If your child knows all of this and more, it will increase his/her chances of doing well on his/her pre-kindergarten test. This test assesses what your child knows or doesn't know before entering kindergarten. This test may also decide what classroom your child is placed in during the fall. Nonetheless, you won't have to worry if you follow the advice in this book, because the tips in this book will help you prepare your child for this pre-test and others like it.

Another thing you can do to make reading exciting and educational is to choose your child's favorite book, and ask him/her who's the author and who's the illustrator. Explain that the illustrator is the person who is responsible for all of the drawings or pictures in the book, and that the author is the one who wrote the book. Next, show your child how you can read the back of a book to get an idea what the book is about. It is also a great way to get your child interested in a story, before you read it to him/her. For an example, let's say you are about to read "Green Eggs and Ham" by Dr. Seuss, you might want to ask your child questions like this: "Do you like green eggs and ham?" or "Who do you think is going to eat those green eggs and ham in the story?" This will encourage your child to listen and pay more attention when you read to him/her. It's a good idea to teach your child to listen and pay attention now, because great listening skills are a plus in school.

Did you know that college is a lot more difficult to get into these days? That is why we have to help our kids do well in school. For an example, here in Georgia we have what we call the Hope (Helping Outstanding Pupils Educationally) Scholarship which is an academic scholarship funded by

The Georgia Lottery. It's allegedly believed that it pays for four years of public/private college/university or technical college in Georgia. To be eligible your son or daughter must allegedly attend a Hope eligible high school, have at least a 3.7 GPA (or higher in the future), be a Georgia resident, and meet other requirements depending on one's circumstances. Please check the requirements at *39.* http://en.wikipedia.org/wiki/HOPE_Scholarship, when your child is ready to begin college, because the requirements may be different then. In any case, as I was mentioning before it is harder for high school graduates to get into college or a university. For instance, go online and take a look at University of Georgia's admission requirements at http://colleges.collegetoolkit.com/colleges/admissions/university_of_georgia/139959.aspx, and you'll find the average GPA (Grade Point Average) of entering high school freshmen is 3.8, and the majority of the entering freshmen have very high ACT and SAT scores, too. Therefore, as you can see the applicants are raising the standards, and colleges and universities are taking the best of the best. Lucky for some of our kids, these colleges/universities are also considering volunteer and work experience, talent and ability, extra-curricular activities, and character/personal qualities. In addition, your child's application essay, recommendations, standardized test scores, high school GPA, and rigor of high school classes will also be taken into consideration. I imagine tougher requirements to get into college are happening all over the country. That is why parents have no other choice but to become more involved in their child's education.

Competition is at an all time high, and we must help our kids compete by preparing them now for the competitive environment they will encounter in the future. That is why this book is so important, because among other things, it will also help parents get their kids ready for college. Parents have to help their kids navigate through this maze called competition. We have to encourage our kids to listen, learn, participate in class, and study at home, because I believe good grades will naturally follow if they do. You should also encourage your kids to do well in music, drama, and in sports, because you never know what natural talents your child may have. It may just help them decide what they want to be when they grow up. You must insist your kids do well in school, so they'll have the qualifications to get into college someday. In my opinion, the more your kids learn, the better they'll do on standardized tests and tests like the SAT and ACT that colleges consider before accepting your child. Besides, don't you want your kids to get into the college of their choice someday? Of course you do. Then, you must persuade your child to learn in school, and to do his/her best in class. We must also give our kids a head start in sports, music, and in other activities, by enrolling them in lessons and different programs that provide additional training in these extra-curricular activities, so your child can compete successfully in the future. Some of you may be thinking, "My child will be fine. He/She will go to college on an academic, sports, or music scholarship." Well, that may just happen (I hope it does), but I don't think it is ever a good idea to put all your eggs in one basket. Kids are smarter, stronger, and more talented these days, and being offered a full academic, sports, or music scholarship, isn't as easy as it has been in the past. Many parents, like you and I, are working hard to give their kids an advantage in everything, too. That is why there's so much competition these days, because there are many parents working with their kids at home to give them the best head start in school, sport, music, and in other activities. That is why I'm writing this book, so that parents everywhere will be inspired to help their kids do their best in school, and encourage them to read and work on educational websites (like the ones mentioned in this book) at home and other skills and talents they may have. Let's face it, things have gotten more competitive, and we have no other choice but to encourage our kids to be excellent at everything, to be put into the race.

Now, that you have a glimpse in what the future may look like, have I motivated you to give your child a real head start, by working with him/her at home? I sure hope so. We have to, if we want our kids to be able to make a decent living in the future. So, what are you waiting for? Start teaching your child everything you can. If you are in a position to give your child music and sport lessons after school, do it. There are other programs we can enroll our kids in like karate, art, a foreign language class, drama, and many others.

I know it all seem a little overwhelming; nevertheless, you have to begin somewhere. So, depending on your child's age and readiness to learn, teach him/her different concepts at home, because remember you are your child's first teacher. Then, regardless of what grade your child is in, continue giving him/her extra schoolwork (that may include the websites in this book, worksheets, extra reading, educational software, etc.) to work on at home, to give him/her a *real* head start in school.

Let's give our kids a real head start by reading lots of books to them, and encourage them to read on their own (if they are reading), because children learn so much from reading. Remember, if you like reading and learning new things, your kids will more than likely be the same way.

When I read as if I'm acting out the story in an enthusiastic way, my kids love it, and the story sounds 10 times more interesting! Therefore, the next time you read a Dr. Seuss book, remember mom and dad, read it as if you're on stage! Just ham it up, and the kids will automatically join in the fun.

If you do not remember anything else in this book, remember this: make it a priority to teach your child how to read, write, and do arithmetic before he/she goes to kindergarten. Then, when he/she is older and starts first grade, you must set some rules around doing homework at home. You must insist on your child completing his/her homework before he/she can play or get on any media or video games. Sometimes, we may have to supervise our kids when they are doing their homework or any extra schoolwork, because kids can become easily distracted. Do visit commonsense. org to learn more on how to improve our kids' life in a 24/7 media and technology world. I've mentioned this before, but parents should put away all iPods, computers, cell phones, video games, etc., until all homework and any extra schoolwork is completed. Don't forget to give your child a break after he/she has completed his/her homework, before giving him/her any extra schoolwork to work on. Keep in mind, your child does not have to complete his/her homework in front of a computer, unless he/she is working on one of the websites mentioned in this book or doing research. Just think about it, he/she may be looking at a video on YouTube.com or checking on his/her Facebook. com account. Why take a chance that your child is wasting his/her time. Remember, what I told you before, kids respect what you inspect.

Remember, if your child is 3 1/2 years old and isn't reading by this stage of the book, and you have followed every step, tip, and suggestion re-teach steps two, three, four, and five. I'm confident that he'll/she'll learn how to read in a little while. In addition to following all of the steps and suggestions in this book, read to your child often, this shows *him/her how to read*. When you're reading to your child, encourage him/her to look at the words you are pointing to as you read. As your child becomes a better reader, remind him/her to follow punctuation rules of periods, commas, exclamation points, and question marks. For instance, if a sentence ends in a period, remind your child to come to a complete stop, before reading the next sentence. If a sentence ends in a question mark, point out that the sentence should be read like someone is asking a question. Next, if a sentence ends in an exclamation point, remind him/her to read it using a very loud voice to put emphasis on something that has gone very right or not so good. Don't forget to remind your child to read stories, as if he/she is acting the story out on stage. Well, if your child is reading go ahead and read the rest of the book, but if he/she hasn't learned to read yet, go to chapters 12 and 13 and re-teach your child steps 2, 3, 4, and 5. After your child has learned to read, you have my blessing to finish reading this book. Feel free to look in the back of the book anytime for the 100+ websites I've mentioned several times throughout the book to have your kids work on. I've labeled each one, to give you an idea what each website focuses on.

Now, that your child is reading (hopefully at this stage in the book), have him/her read to you sometimes. This will give you a chance to listen and praise or correct your child's reading. For instance, if he/she doesn't stop when he/she comes to a period, you can gently remind him/her to stop at all periods, when he/she is reading. In addition, encourage your child to read in an upbeat way and to enunciate every word. This will give your child lots of practice reading sentences the way they *should* be read. If you encourage your child to read with lots of excitement in his/her voice, he/she will naturally read with more inflection in his/her voice. Your child should get plenty of practice just listening to you read. So, remember to read in an upbeat way, follow punctuation rules, and *enunciate*. Sometimes our children are like mimics. They will mimic what we do, therefore, read with lots of energy and mind your punctuation rules.

Another way to encourage your child to read in an upbeat way is to remind him/her to speak that way. If you encourage your child to speak clearly and to enunciate every word every time he talks, he'll/she'll naturally read that way. You might want to point out the punctuation marks as you read, to bring them to his/her attention, so that he'll/she'll pay more attention to them. Teaching children to read with expression is very important, because it's a great way to make everything he/she reads that more interesting. If you find that your child is not good at pausing at commas, stopping at periods, or speaking a little louder when he sees an exclamation point at the end of a sentence, just continue working with him/her at home, until he/she gets the hang of it.

I can't stress it enough, but do read in an upbeat way, because kids notice these types of things. If we're honest, no one likes to listen to anyone who reads in a boring way. So, keep this in mind when you're reading to your child.

The steps and tips in this book will help your child become a conscientious and proficient reader. So, keep asking your child questions when you read to him. It will help him/her with his/her reading comprehension skills. It is also a great way to see if your child is listening to you and understanding what he/she hears or reads on his/her own. So, what are you waiting for? Start implementing some of the strategies in this book today! You'll be glad you did.

CHAPTER XIV

A Word on Teaching Autistic Kids & Closing Remarks

I believe this book can also help autistic children learn to read. I have faith that all kids can learn if we believe in them, and spend a lot of time teaching them different skills that can help them succeed in school. It doesn't matter what doctors or others may think an autistic child can or cannot do, what matters is that his/her family believes in him/her. When you show any child you believe in him/her, it does wonders for his/her self-esteem. A parent who has been told by a doctor or several doctors that their child is autistic (I believe it's always a good idea to get a second or third opinion) should take the news as a challenge, not as if it's the end of the world. I believe an autistic child can make a complete turnaround, if someone works with him/her on a daily basis at home. Therefore, a parent with an autistic child should make it his/her priority to help his/her child learn different things to help him/her overcome autism or minimize its symptoms. In addition, make sure your child that has been diagnosed with autism makes eye contact with family members and others. In addition, parents of an autistic child should focus on his/her strengths and help him/her develop others to diminish the signs of autism. Another great idea is to enroll him/her in a music class or in a sport program that will help him/her grow and develop. All of this and more can make a tremendous impact on your child's development. Furthermore, parents with an autistic child should read to him/her regularly, and ask questions to make sure he/she understands what is happening in the story. It's very important not to mention to your child or anyone else that your child is autistic, because I believe it can make a child feel sorry for himself/herself or give him/her a crutch to lean on. In addition, make sure that others don't treat your child differently either, because it may slow down his/her progress. This is exactly what we don't want to happen. So, remember to treat your child, as if he/she was never diagnosed with autism. Treat your autistic child, as he/she *will be* if you keep working with him/her at home. Besides, to be completely honest, and this is just my opinion--Albert Einstein and Beethoven could have been autistic.

More importantly, if you know parents with an autistic child, and you're sure of it, tell them about this book. I believe it will bless and encourage their family. They can purchase the book at www.amazon.com , and part of the proceeds collected from the sale of each book will go to Literacy, Inc. at http://www.literacyinc.com/donate.html. "Literacy Inc is dedicated to fighting illiteracy in America, especially among our teens. Where our nation's young adults are concerned, the rate of illiteracy is reaching epidemic proportions, and we need your help to reverse this trend. For only $7, you can provide a high school student with books that may lead him or her towards a free college education, " *51.http://www.literacyinc.com/donate.html.*

Concisely, mom and dad, just keep reading, singing, and

teaching your child all sorts of things, and before you know it, your child will be reading, doing arithmetic, writing, drawing, singing and reciting his ABCs and more!

Furthermore, don't forget to encourage retired teachers, professors, doctors, business professionals, and grandparents to volunteer their time and resources to give the kids in their community a real head start in school and in life. It really does take a village to raise a child, which is why it's crucial that we encourage individuals in our neighborhoods to get involved in our kids' education. Everyone can make a difference, because everyone can get involved. Let's show our kids (America's future) that it's important to us that they receive a quality education. So, how does everyone get involved, and change the dialogue from media and technology to education and innovation? Well, here's a hypothetical example: Let's say your neighborhood Chick-fil-A restaurant started rewarding kids for achieving all A's or all A's and B's on their report cards with a kid's meal (after all --what kid doesn't like Chick-fil-A?). Actually, some Chick-fil-A's do reward kids for showing kindness and other great values, but I'm not sure if they reward kids for making good grades in school. Now, to be fair, some businesses and restaurants are rewarding children for their wonderful efforts in school. For an example, some Blockbuster stores reward schoolchildren with all A's on their report card with a free rental on certain videos (call your local Blockbuster store to see if they are participating). Nevertheless, we need everyone on board, and it should start at home and in school. When I was a little girl, my elementary school once a year had a special awards assembly to recognize students with certificates for excelling in certain subjects and for making the honor roll. The whole school attended and your teacher even invited your parents, if you were being rewarded. I felt like a star on those days, because my named was called for every subject. Schools should bring award assemblies back. They should be held at all elementary, middle, and high schools every marking period. I really believe it will motivate all of the students at the school to do their best, especially if we could somehow give out $25.00 Visa gift cards along with every certificate given out, to use at places like the movie theatres, restaurants, bookstores, and the mall. Okay, maybe I went a little over board with the $25.00 gift cards, but putting together an award assembly, shouldn't be out of the question. I'm sure some schools still have them, but I think all schools should start rewarding our kids again for doing well in school, don't you? Let's not forget about our teachers, they should be rewarded for all of their hard work, too.

Now, let's discuss an unpopular subject, and that is when our kids look like our kids, but they're acting like someone else. Well, we must also take into account that sometimes our children are going to have some "less than stellar" moments on their report cards (Really? Yes, really--and sometimes to our surprise). We must take these opportunities (as painful as they may be) and remind our kids why they should do their best in school. If you are thinking of something you can say, just tell them that the reason they should do well in school, is to increase their chances of succeeding in the future. We should also help our kids do their best in school, by hiring a tutor or enrolling them in a learning center. Sometimes, just cheering your child on to make better grades in school, can make a world of difference.

One way to motivate high school students to improve their grades in school is to ask them what they want to be in ten years after graduating because most of them will be at least 27 years old--unbelievable, but true. This can put things in perspective and hopefully inspire your kids to do better in school, so that they can achieve their future goals.

Another idea is to have your child find out the admission requirements of the college he/she wants to go to, so that he/she will know exactly what kind of requirements they are looking for. Here's a tip that will help your child increase his/her chances of making it into college--have him/her apply for early admission. More importantly, we have to encourage our kids to *set goals*, and then motivate them to accomplish them. One of your child's goals may be to be accepted into Georgia Tech. Telling people that you want to attend Georgia Tech after you graduate from high school sounds as impressing as it sounds to tell everyone that you are going to be a doctor when you grow up. Well, I can tell you that it's easier said, than done. That is why I'm encouraging you to have your child research the college of his/her choice. This way he'll/she'll know the requirements necessary to get in, and it should encourage him/her to do better in school. For instance, let's say your child wants to attend Georgia Tech, and the admission requirements for incoming freshmen is allegedly 3.8 Grade Point Average and at least a 1250 on the SAT. The bottom line is that these requirements are tough, yet, they should inspire your child to study for the SAT/ACT test on the weekends and to make excellent grades in 9th -12th grade. This way if your child doesn't make it into Georgia Tech, he'll/she'll at least make it into his/her second or third choice. How do I know? Well, let me explain it in this way. Let's say you have been working extremely hard to bring home a gold medal for our country, but instead, you bring home a silver medal. It isn't a gold medal, but a silver medal is certainly noteworthy, and your efforts should be celebrated. In other words, if you hadn't worked hard enough to earn a gold medal, you might not have earned a silver medal. In contrast, if your child doesn't get into Georgia Tech, but is accepted into another college/university, then at least your child's efforts weren't in vain.

That's why it's so important to have a back up plan, in case your child doesn't make it into his/her first college choice.

Simply put, there is no substitute for hard work. Regardless of what our kids want to be when they grow up, there will always be requirements to meet and tests to take. That's just the way things are. That is why we should support our kids' dreams, but we must also give them the realities behind making those dreams come true. For instance, do you remember the college bound student who went off to college to become a doctor but ended up with a degree in Dietetics Nutrition instead, after changing his degree several times in college? Not that a Dietetics Nutrition degree isn't something to be proud of, but it isn't the doctor degree he initially went to school for, either. So, let's be completely honest with our kids, and encourage them to research the qualifications they will need to accomplish their goals. If we give our kids a roadmap to follow, so to speak, they may just reach their destinations someday. In addition, remind your kids *to get serious* about making it into college or accomplishing their future goals, because accredited colleges/universities/technical colleges aren't accustomed to giving out degrees, they're earned. Accredited degrees are earned, and college bound students are going to have to make up their minds to do their best in school now or simply be left behind.

It's more difficult to get into and excel in college these days, not to mention more expensive. That's another reason we have to encourage our kids to do well in school now *and* in college, so that they will have the skills and credentials, they'll need to get into college and hopefully qualify for a college scholarship. Remember mom and dad, this is the goal-less money out of our pockets-so start cheering your child on today. Why? Well, it is getting more competitive all the time, not only in the classroom, but also on jobs, in sports, in the music and entertainment industry, in politics, and in almost every career you can think of today. At any rate, this is why we must make sure our kids get the best education possible, and we can do this by making sure they read and learn what their schools are trying to teach them and then supplement their education at home.

We have to remind our kids to do their best in school, until they finally realize that education is the key to their dreams. Let me ask you a question. Have you ever met a child who wants to be homeless, depend on public assistance, go to prison, or who didn't want to become successful in the future? Of course, you haven't. Every child dreams of becoming somebody great; therefore, it's up to us to help our kids get a quality education in grades K-12th and encourage them to go to college/technical school or into the service after graduating from high school. Keep in mind, some of our kids won't follow the traditional path mentioned above, and will succeed on their own terms. Some of our kids may want to become entertainers and start Juilliard School after graduation, and some of them may want to become professional chefs and study at a Culinary School in Paris. Some of our kids are creative, and they'll grow up to be writers, movie directors and producers, designers, and so much more! Some of our kids were born to be professional athletes and some of them will probably start playing professional ball after high school or college. Last, but not least, some of our kids are innovators who will create and build businesses of their own, like Bill Gates, Steve Jobs, and Oprah Winfrey--just to name a few. They are extraordinary individuals, and they make a world of difference in our world.

Well, regardless of what our kids decide to become let's help them achieve their goals by encouraging them to write down their goals and to go after them with all their might.

If we encourage our kids everyday to do their best in school, they will grow up to be happy, responsible, and law abiding citizens.

I know teachers care and are accountable for what our kids learn in class, but when it's over and done with-- what your child *really learns* in and out of class will ultimately be up to you and your child. Therefore, persuade your child to listen and learn in school, as well as do his/her homework and study for all tests and quizzes. One way to make sure your child is prepared for tests and quizzes is to have him/her read assigned chapters and to learn the boldly printed vocabulary words that accompanies each chapter. In addition, make sure your child completes the chapter assessment that goes with each chapter, before taking all tests and quizzes. Another great idea is to have your child complete all chapter review sessions on the textbook's website. Did you know most textbooks have websites that provide additional study material that can help your child do well on tests and quizzes? If you're not sure where to find your child's textbook's website, just send the teacher an email and ask him/her or look at the front of your child's textbook.

Make sure you teach your child some sensible things, too. For instance, teach your child how to count his/her change, to make sure that the cashier gave him/her back the right amount. Another thing you can teach your child to do is how to figure out the cost of a gallon of gas. What you're actually doing is teaching your child to pay attention to his/her surroundings, because believe it or not, your child can learn many things, by just paying attention to everyday life. Here are some other real life examples you can do with your child. Encourage your child to help you with a few recipes in the kitchen. All of the measuring and mixing is like doing science and math. He/She can also help you sort the laundry by matching socks (putting like things together-that's math, too). You can encourage your child to help you with the grocery shopping, and that's reading and math, because you may have to count out apples and read to know which aisle to go down. Whatever you do, just remember to take every opportunity to teach your child something new. These are moments, I like to call "teachable moments".

If your child is in high school (9th to 12th grade), give them assignments from edhelper.com throughout the school year and during the summer. This is a wonderful website for all grade levels, and you can print off worksheets to have your child work on. Don't forget to have him/her work on his/her vocabulary by completing at least one lesson a day on www.wordlywise.com. Overall, both of these websites and the others mentioned in the back of this book, can help you give your child a real head start in school and keep him/her ahead.

If your child is a new reader, use every opportunity to encourage him/her to read words on billboards, church bulletin boards, road signs, bumper stickers (the good ones--of course), and including all the words you can find throughout a supermarket. These are great things to do with your child, because I did these things with my son, and he took it a step further, and started memorizing the names and operation times of restaurants and other businesses on his own. He kept track of when they opened and closed. His natural curiosity about how things work in the world made him a walking database. It also set the stage for him to become a good student in school. He still uses those memorization skills and his inquisitiveness to learn today. So, keep encouraging your child to learn all he/she can learn, regardless if he/she is at home, at school, or out and about.

You should also encourage your child to read all the time. The more he/she reads, the smarter he'll/she'll become-- and the smarter he/she becomes, the more he/she will grow, evolve, and become. In addition, you should encourage your child to read books on a number of different subjects, but you should also remind him/her to read game instructions, directions, advertisements, stories about other kids, autobiographies, and certainly bible stories. Furthermore, "Highlights" is a great children's magazine your child should want to read on his/her own. It is filled with lots of stories, poems, and puzzles. Another attention-grabbing magazine to encourage your child to read is an online magazine called The National Geographic. This magazine can be found at http://kids.nationalgeographic.com/kids. This website is also an excellent way to expose your child to science, social studies, and geography.

Of course, if your child isn't reading yet, don't give up on him/her. Just continue working with your child until he/she does learn to read. You'll know the moment your child learns to read, because he'll/she'll being to recognize simple sight words, like the ones mentioned in Chapter 12, and he'll/she'll start to pronounce them on his/her own. As your child's reading progresses, he'll/she'll begin to sound out words he/she isn't familiar with, as well. In any case, enjoy this journey as your child learns to read words like "The", "cat", "is", "in", and "house" and sentences like this one derived from the words just cited, "The cat is in the house."

You can also give your child a real head start in other things, like sports. For an example, it's not enough to just enroll your child in sports, and expect the coach to do everything. If you want your child to do well on game day, work with him/her at home. You can even enroll your child in different sport programs during the summer, to help him/her hone his/her skills during the off-season.

Nowadays, many parents are investing a lot of time and

money to give their kids the best head start in school, music, drama, dance, and in sports. Consequently, these are the kids who are raising the bar in schools, sports, music, and so much more! That is why I wrote this book to encourage all parents to give their kids the same kind of head start (if not better) without paying a whole lot of money. If you aren't teaching your child something new or helping him/her sharpen a natural talent you've discovered he/she has, you could potentially be giving him/her a false start. If you use the tips and strategies in this book *consistently*, your child is going to get a *real* head start in school and a jump-start on his/her dreams.

I can't stress this enough, but I'm going to say it again anyway. Teach your child how to read yourself, because reading is one of those skills that your child will use in church, at school, at home, and in his/her future profession. Reading will always be present in our lives; it's a lifelong skill and a necessary one.

It's a great thing you're teaching your child how to read early, too, because according to research, adults who cannot read have problems reading restaurant menus and bus schedules. As cited before here is some research that shows fourteen countries above us in reading ability. In addition, there are 65,000 adults in Buffalo, New York alone that cannot read above a 5th grade level, and recently there has been an increase in adult illiteracy in California, New York, and Florida. *(23. Source: CBS Evening News Jan. 9, 2009)* This is unbelievable--but so true!

So, do everything in your power to give your kids a *real* head start in school and continue working with them at home to keep them ahead. One of the reasons we have to work with our kids at home is because our kids are taught new concepts in school so quickly, that our kids hardly get anytime to learn them. In most cases, our kids are introduced to a new concept on Monday, and by next Monday, they are on a new subject. Therefore, that is why we must give our kids extra schoolwork to practice what they learn in school, so that they will retain what they learn. Then, when they take tests like the CRCT, ITBS, SAT, ACT, PSAT, and other standardized tests they'll be prepared to take them.

According to Alliance for Excellent Education, "Every year, approximately 1.2 million students—that is 7,000 every school day—*do not graduate from high school on time.* Nationwide, only about 70 percent of students earn their high school diplomas. Among minority students, only 57.8 percent of Hispanic, 53.4 percent of African American, and 49.3 percent of American Indian and Alaska Native students in the U.S. graduate with a regular diploma, compared to 76.2 percent of Caucasian students and 80.2 percent of Asian Americans." *(24. http://www.all4ed.org/about_the_crisis)* For the sake of America, we must encourage our neighbors, friends, and family members to make learning a priority in their homes. Better yet, buy everyone you know a copy of this book, and encourage them to give the children in their lives a real head start in life.

More importantly, remember that you are your child's first teacher, and teaching them as much as you can while he/she is young, is one of the smartest things you can do for your child.

Finally, we must encourage and motivate our kids to work hard in school everyday. I know I have mentioned this before, but it's certainly worth repeating, because our kids have what it takes to make good grades in school and to graduate from high school *on time.* The head start tips in this book can and will give your child the kind of foundation he'll/she'll need in each grade to succeed in school and go on to accomplish his/her goals in the future.

Well, I've come to the end of this book, and I hope

I have encouraged you to teach your child how to read, write, and to do arithmetic early. I hope I have motivated you to remind your child to respect his/her elders at school (including teachers, principals, janitors and the cafeteria staff). I hope I've convinced you to give your child "a real head start" in school and to keep him/her ahead in grades kindergarten through 12th grade. I hope you enroll your child in different sport programs, music lessons, as well as, take him/her to the library, museums, aquariums, planetariums, and amusement parks. I hope I have encouraged you to feed your child healthier. One way you can do this is to put out a small platter of fruit and veggies with low fat Ranch dressing on the side at every meal. If your kids grab at least seven a meal, that's more than they would have eaten. Make sure all snacks and meals consist of whole grains, fiber, lean protein (fish, turkey, and skinless chicken) lots of fish, and low fat dairy products. Make sure your child gets plenty of rest and exercise, too. Encourage your kids to behave in public and in private, because as the old saying goes, "How we act when we think no one is watching is who we really are". Remind your kids to listen in class, and not to talk when the teacher is speaking. I also hope I've inspired you to read often to your child, and to encourage him/her to read regularly, too. In addition, I hope I have inspired you to use the resources in your community and websites referenced in this book to supplement your child's education.

In closing, I can't tell you how much I've enjoyed sharing these tested secrets with you, and I'm confident that your child will get "a real head start in school and in some other areas" as you put the tips and strategies of this book into practice. Remember to visit my website www.realheadstart. com for more tips and strategies on giving your child a *real* head start in everything.

I certainly hope you stay in touch with me, and I

would love to hear about your child's successes. So, email me anytime at realheadstart@gmail.com or follow me on Twitter.com/EducateEarly to tell me all about your child's accomplishments (Who knows you and your child may be selected to appear on my website.), or to share another great website that can give our kids a real head start in school and in life.

Well, don't forget to look for other books by me in the future. Good luck and I wish you and your child much success now and in the future!

Samantha W. Davis

100+ Websites to Keep Your Child Smart and Competitive

1. www.edhelper.com
   great learning site for reading, math, science, etc. small fee to join edhelper.com

2. www.webkinz.com
   get free code with a webkinz plush toy lots of learning under Quizzy's corner once you log on

3. http://www.sheppardsoftware.com/
   lots of brain games

4. www.ixl.com
   all about math up to 8th grade

5. www.multiplication.com
   all about multiplication

6. http://www.brainquest.com/kids
   trivia questions

7. www.Bigiqkids.com
   click on premium programs to sign up—there is a fee to use this site (but worth it) spelling and more!

8. http://abcteach.com/directory/basics/handwriting/
   hand writing practice

9. http://www.tlsbooks.com/firstgradeworksheets.htm
free learning work sheets up to 5th grade

10. http://cbhministries.org/kfk/home.php
family devotions

11. http://abcteach.com/
lots of learning work sheets—there is a small fee to use this website

12. http://quizlet.com/
best way to learn vocabulary and languages

13. http://www.merriam-webster.com/
the dictionary

14. http://www.unclefred.com/
easy drawing lessons

15. http://www.vocabtest.com/
vocabulary builder

16. http://www.funtrivia.com/quizzes/history/us_history.html
about U.S. History

17. www.brainetics.com
math memory system—a fee is associated with this program

18. http://www.boardman.k12.oh.us/bdms/golubic/dolch.htm
word builder

19. http://kids.nationalgeographic.com/kids/
about animals and more

20. www.funbrain.com
learning fun

21. http://www.pbs.org/teachers
great teaching videos for kids

22. www.jumpstart.com
    jump start on skills

23. Yahooligans.yahoo.com
    Yahoo fun for kids—Study Break!

24. www.nick.com
    Nick. Fun for kids—Study Break!

25. www.kbears.com
    some learning fun!

26. www.kids.gov
    government for kids and more!

27. http://www.monroe.lib.in.us/childrens/kidswebs.html
    websites for kids

28. http://bensguide.gpo.gov/subject.html
    U.S. government fun for kids

29. www.starfall.com
    ABC's and reading fun

30. http://www.kidsites.com/sites-edu/math.htm
    all about math

31. http://www.4kids.org/
    trivia for kids

32. http://kidsedwebsites.com/
    interactive learning for kids

33. http://www.kids321.com/home.php
    learning, games, and activities for kids!

34. http://www.nasa.gov/audience/forkids/kidsclub/flash/index.html
    NASA's learning website

35. www.brentwood.k12.ca.us/brentwood/Links/
DolchProject/index.html
more word practice

36. http://www.teach-nology.com/worksheets/language_arts/
dolch/
great learning work sheets

37. http://www.mrcpl.org/literacy/lessons/sight/index.html
literacy fun for kids

38. http://www.netrover.com/~crose/dolch/dolch.htm
word games

39. http://funschool.kaboose.com/
fun learning for kids

40. http://www.learn4good.com/kids/index.htm
learning sites

41. http://www.theteachersguide.com/interactivesites.html
learning interactive sites

42. http://www.gamequarium.com/
learning fun

43. http://www.surfnetkids.com/
online learning games

44. http://www.thekidzpage.com/
learning pages

45. http://www.learningplanet.com/stu/index.asp
math up to 7th grade plus

46. http://www.uni.edu/becker/Spanish3.html
learn Spanish

47. http://www.freeworksheets.com/
free work sheets

48. www.dineydigitalbooks.com
Disney books

49. http://www.clicknkids.com/Phonics.asp
reading learning site

50. http://www.kidsknowit.com/interactive-educational-movies/index.php
learning videos

51. http://www.kristensguide.com/Family/Fun_Kid_Stuff/kid_sites.asp
great websites for kids

52. http://www.enchantedlearning.com/Home.html
the learning pages

53. http://jc-schools.net/tutorials/interact-read.htm
interactive reading websites

54. www.nickjr.com
games and activities from Nick jr.

55. www.brainpop.com
all about science and more

56. http://www.greatschools.org/
teaching tips and more

57. http://www.prongo.com/
education games for ages 3 to 12

58. http://www.miamiopia.com/
all about science & math

59. http://www.activityvillage.co.uk/
printables and more

60. http://www.marks-english-school.com/games.html
about English

61. http://www.scholastic.com/kids/stacks/books/
about books

62. http://www.bookadventure.com/
about reading

63. http://www.minsocam.org/msa/k12/k_12.html
about rocks

64. http://www.multiplication.com/
about multiplication

65. http://www.exploratorium.edu/
explore science

66. http://thekidzpage.com/
online learning games

67. http://zula.com/
discovery fun

68. http://www.plcmc.org/bookhive/
about books

69. http://www.roythezebra.com/reading-games-word-level.html
interactive reading games

70. http://www.spartechsoftware.com/reeko/
science lab

71. http://books.google.com/
all about books

72. http://www.tumblebooks.com/
different books for all ages

73. http://www.yourchildlearns.com/lettersounds.htm
letter & sounds

74. http://www.yourchildlearns.com/puzzle_us.htm
about puzzles

75. http://www.yourchildlearns.com/color-letters.html
about letters

76. http://www.umass.edu/aesop/fables.php
more stories to read

77. http://americanfolklore.net/
different stories

78. http://www.spellingcity.com/
about spelling and more

79. http://www.abcya.com/
where learning & technology meets

80. http://www.learninggamesforkids.com/math_games.html
math games

81. http://www.wacona.com/kindergartengames/
kindergartengames.html
learning for pre-kindergartners or kindergartners

82. http://www.knowledgeadventure.com/
education games

83. http://www.fisher-price.com/fp.aspx?
st=10&e=gamesLanding&mcat=gam
e_infant,game_toddler,game_preschool&site=us
preschool games

84. http://skydiary.com/kids/
all about storms

85. http://www.weatherwizkids.com/
about weather

86. http://whyfiles.org/021climate/index.html
all about the earth's climate

87. http://www.nws.noaa.gov/om/reachout/kidspage.shtml
about weather

102. http://www.storyplace.org/
      about books

103. http://www.americanliterature.com/booktitleindex.html
      about reading

104. www.wordlywise.com
      build your child's vocabulary

105. http://www.realheadstart.com
      the book's website & more education tips

106. http://twitter.com/educateearly
      follow me on Twitter

107. http://www.storiestogrowby.com/
      stories to read

Disclaimer: All websites referenced throughout this book, are for reference purposes. If the website is not found or no longer exists, please do a google or internet search. There is always the possibility that a website address may have been moved or renamed.

References

1. THE HOLY BIBLE: NEW INTERNATIONAL VERSION: Matthew 19:26 (Chapter 1)
2. Atlanta Journal Constitution: http://blogs.ajc.com/get-schooled-blog/2010/05/23/class-size-after-state-board-vote-monday-the-skys-the-limit/ (Chapter 1)
3. http://www.youtube.com/watch?v=pUm1j-ScXIs (Chapter 1)
4. National Center for Education Standards (Chapter 1)
5. The Daily Encouraging Word (Chapter 4)
6. Don't Know Much About The Presidents: Davis, Kenneth C. China: Harper Collins Publishers, ©2002. (Chapter 5)
7. THE HOLY BIBLE: NEW INTERNATIONAL VERSION: Proverbs (Chapter 8)
8. Kidspeace.org (Chapter 8)
9. GOD'S WORD ® Translation: Psalms 127:3 (Chapter 8)
10. Introducing Your Baby to Books While In the Womb Isn't As Stupid As It Sounds by Terry Ross: http://ezinearticles.com (Chapter 8)
11. Does classical music make babies smarter? By Denise Winterman BBC News Magazine (Chapter 9)
12. www.musicmindspirit.org, quoted on http://www.itummy.net/references.php (Chapter 9)
13. http://www.askamum.co.uk/Pregnancy/Search-Results/Week-by-week/How-is-your-baby-developing-in-the-womb/ (Chapter 9)

14. http://en.wikipedia.org/wiki/Mozart_effect (Chapter 9)
15. Indiana.edu: Human Intelligence Mozart Effect www. indiana.edu/~intell/mozarteffect2.shtml. (Chapter 9)
16. The National Right To Read Foundation (Chapter 9)
17. http://today.msnbc.msn.com/id/36126004/ns/today-today_books/ (Chap. 10)
18. 1 Samuel 16:7 NIV (Chap. 10)
19. What Is Your Life's Blueprint?: http://seattletimes. nwsource.com/special/mlk/king/words/blueprint.html Six months before he was assassinated, King spoke to a group of students at Barratt Junior High School in Philadelphia on October 26, 1967 (Chap. 10)
20. Dr. Thomas Verny, the Secret Life of the Unborn Child (Chap. 11)
21. Dr. Thomas Verny-Author of The Secret Life of the Unborn Child (Chap. 11)
22. Dr. Thomas Verny, the Secret Life of the Unborn Child (Chap. 11)
23. CBS Evening News Jan. 9, 2009 (Chap. 15)
24. http://www.all4ed.org/about_the_crisis (Chap. 15)
25. Quote from Diane Dew at http://www.dianedew.com/ runrace.htm) (Chap.8)
26. http://sga.astate.edu/Documents/EventsInfo/ Lottery%20Research.pdf
27. http://www.dianedew.com/runrace.htm (Chap.1)
28. http://www.infoplease.com/ipa/A0923110.html (Chap. 2)
29. Precious Moments Bible (Chap. 4)
30. Precious Moments Bible (Chap. 4)
31. Heb. 12:1-3; http://bible.cc/hebrews/12-1.htm (Chap. 8)
32. (2 Thessalonians 4:7-8); http://bible.cc/2_timothy/4-8. htm (Chap. 8)
33. (Heb 12: 1-3)." (Quoted from http://www.dianedew. com/runrace.htm) (Chap. 8)

34. (http://sga.astate.edu/Documents/EventsInfo/
    Lottery%20Research.pdf) (Chap. 8)
35. (http://sga.astate.edu/Documents/EventsInfo/
    Lottery%20Research.pdf) (Chap. 8)
36. http://www.associatedcontent.com/article/738155/
    movie_ratings_meanings_for_parents.html (Chap.9)
37. http://www.19actionnews.com/Global/story.asp?S=138
    65892&clienttype=printable (Chap. 9)
38. NIV©1984 http://bible.cc/luke/6-31.htm (Chap. 9)
39. http://en.wikipedia.org/wiki/HOPE_Scholarship
    (Chap. 13)
40. http://www.ehow.com/facts_5183402_do-sports-
    kids_.html (Chap.2)
41. http://musiced.about.com/od/beginnersguide/a/pinst.
    htm (Chap. 2)
42. http://www.huffingtonpost.com/2010/05/09/obama-
    at-hampton-universi_n_569258.html
43. Microsoft Word Processor; (Chapter 6)
44. Microsoft Word Processor; (Chapter 6)
45. http://www.2theadvocate.com/news/education/
    19520584.html and Essence Magazine 2010 (Chap.13)
46. http://www.2theadvocate.com/news/education/
    19520584.html and Essence Magazine 2010 (Chap. 13)
47. http://en.wikipedia.org/wiki/American_Dream (Chap.1)
48. http://www.huffingtonpost.com/2010/05/09/obama-
    at-hampton-universi_n_569258.html (Chap. 4)
49. http://ezinearticles.com/?Introducing-Your-Baby-To-
    Books-While-In-The-Womb-Isnt-As-Stupid-As-It-
    Sounds&id=305709
50. http://www.bigy.com/education/hwhl.php
51. http://www.literacyinc.com/donate.html
52. http://www.youtube.com/watch?v=vitqaJ7VKqQ&feat
    ure=related